HOW TO FIGHT A BEAR ...AND WIN

& 72 OTHER SURVIVAL TIPS WE HOPE YOU'LL NEVER NEED

"There were all kinds of things I was afraid of at first, ranging from grizzly bears to mean horses and gunfighters. But by acting as if I was not afraid I gradually ceased to be afraid."

—Teddy Roosevelt

"I believe all creatures have a soul. Except bears. Bears are godless killing machines!"

—Stephen Colbert

UNCLE JOHN'S
HOW TO FIGHT A BEAR AND WIN

Copyright © 2015 by Portable Press.

Portable Press/The Bathroom Readers' Institute
An imprint of Printers Row Publishing Group
P.O. Box 1117, Ashland, OR 97520
www.bathroomreader.com
e-mail: mail@bathroomreader.com

Printers Row Publishing Group is a division of
Readerlink Distribution Services, LLC.

The Portable Press, Bathroom Readers' Institute, and Uncle John's Bathroom Reader names and logos are trademarks of Readerlink Distribution Services, LLC.

All correspondence concerning the content of this book should be addressed to Portable Press/The Bathroom Readers' Institute, Editorial Department, at the above address.

Cover design by Andy Taray (ohioboy.com)
Illustrations by Tom Deja (bossmangraphics.com)
Interior design by Lidija Tomas

Library of Congress Cataloging-in-Publication Data
Uncle John's how to fight a bear and win.
   pages cm
 ISBN 978-1-62686-421-4 (hardcover)
1. Survival--Humor. 2. American wit and humor. I. Bathroom Readers' Institute (Ashland, Or.) II. Title: How to fight a bear and win.
   PN6231.S886U53 2015
   818'.602--dc23

               2014041900

Printed in the United States of America
First Printing: October 2015
19 18 17 16 15   1 2 3 4 5

THANK YOU!

*The Bathroom Readers' Institute sincerely thanks
the people whose advice and assistance
made this book possible.*

Gordon Javna

Brian Boone

Tom Deja

Lidija Tomas

Trina Janssen

Andy Taray

Christy Taray

Brandon Hartley

Jack Feerick

Pablo Goldstein

Ben Godar

Julie McLaughlin

Megan Todd

Jay Newman

Dan Mansfield

Kim Griswell

Aaron Guzman

Rusty von Dyl

J. Carroll

Shea Strauss

David Hoye

Jennifer and Mana

Melinda Allman

Peter Norton

Lilian Nordland

CONTENTS

STAYIN' ALIVE!

It's not just the name of Uncle John's favorite song—it's job no. 1 for anyone who's ever found themselves stuck in the woods, desert, or any other place far from food, shelter, and safety.

That's why we created *How to Fight a Bear and Win*. Herein, you'll find everything you need to know to get by in the Great Outdoors. Yes, you'll learn how to build a fire, and what plants you can eat. But you'll *also* learn...

• How to calm a wild moose
• How to swing from a vine like Tarzan
• How to cut off your arm if it's stuck under a rock
• And lots, lots more.

Of course, we hope you're never in a situation where you need to apply anything you read in *How to Fight a Bear and Win*, but if you do, good luck out there...and sorry.

**—Uncle John and the
Bathroom Readers' Institute**

HOW TO MAKE FIRE

It's actually illegal to publish a survival book—even a semi-facetious one—without including a section on all the different ways you can make fire.

THE HAND DRILL METHOD

This way is a bit time-consuming, but it should get the job done. First, you'll need some tinder, or flammable material that will help you build a fire. Dry bark and leaves work great, as do cattails, if you can find them. Gather some dry kindling and firewood while you're at it. Once you have all of these supplies, return to your campsite and prepare a circular fire pit. Prepare a "tinder nest" in the center, a small circle comprising broken-up tinder.

Next, find a small, flat piece of wood that will serve as your "fireboard." Cut a small V-shaped notch in the center and place

11

the board over a piece of dry bark. Grab a "spindle stick" (a sturdy stick about two feet long) and place one end in the notch. Quickly roll the stick between your hands while making sure that it's firm against the board. The friction should create a smoldering ember...a few minutes after, you'll start to think about giving up because it's taking so much time and effort to get a spark. Quickly move it to the bark and place the ember in the tinder nest. Blow gently on the ember to keep it smoldering, and then prepare another ember. Repeat the process until the nest catches on fire. Add the kindling and, when the flames are going, the wood. Fire!

THE FLINT AND STEEL METHOD

You'll need a sharp metal "striker" for this one. A steel knife is ideal, but you can also use a flat tin can or a sharpened belt buckle. You'll also need a "flint rock" (a round rock with jagged edges) and something that will serve as a "char cloth." This can be a flat bit of charcoal from an old fire, dried tree fungus, or even paper if you have any (such as the parts of this book you've already read). Prepare a tinder nest in your fire pit, as described above. Place the cloth and the rock in the same hand and quickly scrape the striker against it. Needless to say, you should be careful to avoid stabbing yourself with it. If you hit the rock just right, it should emit a spark. Keep doing this until one ignites the cloth. Transport the now-flaming cloth to your tinder nest and, once it catches on fire, add the kindling and then the wood when the time is right. Fire!

THE SHERLOCK METHOD

You've probably heard that a magnifying glass can serve as a fire-making tool, or perhaps you were the kind of child who lit ants on fire in this manner. Well, it works! Just place the magnifying glass over a tinder  nest on a sunny day, and a sunbeam will eventually shine through and ignite it. You can also use binoculars and eyeglasses. Fire!

THE ICE METHOD

First, you'll need a chunk of clear ice—one that's cloudy or has too much dirt inside it won't work. The simplest way to create the ideal ice for this method is to freeze some water overnight in a cup or another container. Place just enough water in it to form a two-inch chunk. Using a knife or sharp edge, shape it into a lens and polish it with a cloth (the end of your shirt should work). Then prepare a tinder nest in your fire pit, point your new ice lens toward the sun, and let the awesome powers of thermodynamics work their magic. Fire!

THE SODA CAN METHOD

Make a tinder nest, and polish the bottom of the can until it's shiny. Use the polished can to reflect the sun's rays onto the nest. This will take longer (and will probably be considerably more frustrating)  than the Ice Method, but with enough time and patience, you should have a roaring fire to keep you toasty warm.

HOW TO FIND WATER IN THE DESERT AND DRINK IT

There isn't a lot of water in the desert—that's kind of the desert's "thing." However, if you're trapped out there for whatever reason, your human need for water doesn't go away. Here's how to get it, and then what to do with it so you can drink it.

SEEK IT OUT

1. Desert plants such as cottonwoods, willows, sycamores, and cattails grow near groundwater.

2. Where there's wildlife, there's probably water. Watch where birds go, and follow them. Bees are also a great way to find water—they'll swarm in a straight line to and from a water source up to half a mile away.

3. Dry streams and riverbeds are not always completely dry. Dig around, and you might find dampness a few inches down.

4. Keep digging the hole, and water will seep into it.

5. Moisture can accumulate under rocks. Turn over every stone, literally. (Watch out for scorpions, though—scorpions are scorpions, not water.)

6. Do the dew! Look for dewdrops that accumulate on plants and flowers before dawn, sop up the moisture with a cloth, and then wring out the cloth into a container. The undersides of rocks may have some dew on them as well.

7. While it's true that water can be taken from cacti, it's not true of *all* cacti. Some cacti offer a milky liquid—don't drink that, because it's poisonous. The prickly pear cactus is the one to look for, because it offers up actual water.

SUMMON IT

Making a solar still is a way to force water to condense into your very own water container. Here's how to do it.

1. Locate a dried-out riverbed, like in the previous section. Dig a hole about 20 inches deep, until you've reached the subsoil. If you're lucky, it might be a little moist. (Note: do not do this in a shady spot, or where shade may occur when the sun changes positions in the sky. You'll need direct sunlight for this to work.)

2. Pee in the hole, just a little. (Look, this provides a bit of "starter moisture," okay?)

3. Throw any green plants you can find into the hole.

4. In the center of the hole, with the plants around it, place a mug, cup, or coffee can.

5. Place a layer of plastic wrap across the top of the hole, completely covering it.

6. Seal the hole. Pour sand in a circle around the edge of the plastic wrap. Secure it more by placing rocks around the edge. It has to be completely sealed for the water to condense.

7. Place a small rock on the top of the wrap, in the center. You want the rock to weigh down the wrap so it dips to just above, but not touching, the mug or can in the hole.

8. The sun's heat will cause water to evaporate out of the moist soil and the plants in the hole. Since the water cannot escape the sealed hole, it will condense on the wrap, and then drip into the can.

PURIFY IT

*However you get that water, you might want to
clean it up, just to be on the safe side.*

1. Allow cloudy water to settle before filtering.

2. Cut off a pant leg. (You'll need about half of
    it.) It's hot in the desert—why are you even
    still wearing long pants anyway?

3. Tie off the bottom of the leg tightly with
    string or twine, or just form it into a knot.

4. Hang the pant leg off a tree branch and place
    a catch basin underneath. A cup will do
    nicely.

5. Fill the sealed pant leg with alternating layers
    of small rocks and sand: rocks, sand, rocks,
    sand, rocks. Leave about half an inch of room
    at the top.

6. Slowly and carefully pour water into the top.
    It will pool, but then slowly trickle through
    the layers, which will trap bad debris, and
    then flow into the cup.

7. Now boil it.

HOW TO GET OUT OF A CAR TRUNK YOU'RE LOCKED IN

A Mafia hit, an abduction for ransom, a family reunion gone awry—there are all sorts of reasons why you might end up locked in a car trunk.

HOW TO DO IT

1. **Stay calm.** No trunk is completely airtight, so you're not going to suffocate—but if you panic, you may hyperventilate.

2. **Kill the lights.** If you've been abducted and feel your life is in immediate danger, it's more important to summon help than to actually get out. One way to surreptitiously do this is to disable the car's taillights, which you can do from inside the trunk. You may have to pry off a plastic cover to access the taillight assembly; once you do, push or kick until the lights pop out. Look through the hole to ascertain your location. If you're

in a populated area, stick your hand out to wave at passing motorists or, hopefully, law enforcement.

3. **Look for the lever.** As a child safety measure, all late-model cars manufactured in the U.S. have a release latch inside the trunk, designed to be easy enough for a three-year-old—or a panicked adult—to find and operate. Some even have handles that glow in the dark. Failing that, older cars often have a lever under the dashboard that lets the driver pop the trunk. This connects to the lock via a cable running along the driver's side. Pull up the carpet or sheathing and feel around for the cable. Grip firmly and pull toward the front of the car.

4. **Work the latch.** A savvy kidnapper may disable the safety lever and the remote release. In this case, you must force the lock manually. Trunk locks are usually a simple assembly, a single latch that pivots to catch on a bolt or rod. Push against the hook end of the latch with enough force, and it will swing free. It's not really a job you can do

bare-handed, though; grope around in the trunk for tools. Pry up the chipboard floor panel, and you might find a crowbar or jack-handle that will do the trick. And just in case you get caught trying to free yourself, a good solid tire iron in your hand will give you more confidence in dispatching your abductor.

5. **Tuck and roll.** Time your escape. Estimate the speed of the car. The best time to get out is when the car is rolling slowly, rather than at a dead stop. Wait until the car begins to slow to make your move; pop the latch, push upward in one smooth motion, and scramble out of the trunk. Landing on your feet may not be an option; try to take the impact on your shoulder, protecting your head, and roll toward the passenger side, out of traffic. Get to your feet as quickly as you can and head for safety.

HOW TO BUILD A CANOE OUT OF A TREE

Well, now you've done it. You're stranded on an island in the middle of a lake, or possibly a river, with nothing but a downed tree and a few hand tools. So build yourself a boat and get back to the mainland.

WHAT YOU'LL NEED

- A tree trunk, wider than you at your widest place

- An axe, adze, or some other primitive chopping tool
- Fire!

HOW TO DO IT

1. The trunk needs to be wide enough for you to sit in it comfortably, so the diameter should be 6 to 12 inches larger than your posterior. Length can vary, but a good rule of thumb is to make sure it's long enough that you can

lie down in it. Because you're only working with a primitive chopping tool, it's best to find a tree that's already down. (Tip: Make sure the downed tree you use isn't already rotten. While it would be much easier to hollow out, it would also likely disintegrate in the water, leaving you "up a creek," literally and figuratively.)

2. You don't need to get too elaborate, but you will need to do a bit of basic shaping to turn this tree into a boat. Hack off the ends (if necessary) to get the trunk to the appropriate length. Remove any bark from the tree. Finally, chop along one side of the trunk to create a flat bottom for your boat. The flat bottom will prevent the boat from rolling and dumping you into the water.

3. Using your adze, hack away into what will be the top of your boat, until you've dug out a trough a few inches deep and about a foot wide.

4. In the trough you created, start a small fire. You could use kindling, although charcoal is

ideal because the fire will need to continue burning for hours, if not days.

5. Scrape out the charred wood. Periodically, as a section of the trunk has softened and charred, you will want to stop or move the fire and scrape out the charred wood.

6. Repeat steps 4 and 5 until the trunk is hollowed out. Proceed slowly—if the entire log catches fire, you will have a bonfire instead of a boat.

7. Cover the outside of the boat in tree sap. The tree sap will serve as a lacquer and partially waterproof your new boat. Voilà! You made a boat!

HOW NOT TO BLEED TO DEATH

Blood is the substance of life, but it only works properly if it stays where it belongs: inside of you.

UNDER PRESSURE

1. The best bandage is your blood's own clotting factor. A clot is like the skin on a bowl of soup that's been left out too long; it won't form if the broth is still bubbling. Direct pressure can pinch off the ruptured vessel and let the blood pool long enough to coagulate.

2. Raise the wound above the heart and press down steadily just above the wound with a sterile gauze pad or clean cloth.

3. If the gauze soaks through, don't remove it, as this could pull away the fresh scab. Just add a fresh pad atop the soaked one, and keep up the pressure.

TIE IT OFF

1. If direct pressure does not stanch the bleeding, cut off circulation to the wounded limb with a tourniquet. Twine or wire can bite into the skin and make matters worse; try a shirtsleeve, belt, or backpack strap.

2. Tie your tourniquet between the heart and the wound, using an overhand knot; leave the ends free.

3. Put a stout stick atop the knot, tie it in place, and twist in one direction to tighten the tourniquet.

KILL IT WITH FIRE

1. Cauterization is a last resort for wounds that will not otherwise stop bleeding. It works by using heat to denature the proteins in your blood, causing it to coagulate. It's also very risky to do by yourself, because you will severely burn the surrounding skin and are almost sure to get a secondary infection. But if your life's on the line, you can reduce

the risk by using a topical disinfectant—like alcohol—both before and after the procedure, and keeping the burned area covered with antibiotic ointment and a sterile bandage.

2. The best instrument for cauterization is the flat of a knife blade. Heat your instrument to just below the point where it glows red. (Whatever you've seen in the movies, don't use gunpowder; it burns far too hot, and will destroy more tissue than it saves.)

3. Touch the heated implement lightly to the wound for a few seconds at a time until the bleeding stops, reheating periodically if necessary.

4. Seek professional medical attention at your earliest opportunity.

HOW TO AVOID A TORNADO

If you got swept up by a tornado, cyclone, dust devil, twister, whirlwind, or whatever else you want to call it, there's a very small chance you'll wind up in Oz. A more likely scenario is that you'll spin around in the sky for a while and get dumped in a field, hard. Here's how to sit out the storm.

THE WINDS OF CHANGE

• First, be aware when you're in a tornado-prone area. Almost all tornadoes in the U.S. touch down in "Tornado Alley," a region that extends from the Deep South, up through the Plains states, into the Southwest, and as far north as Canada.

• If you live in or are visiting Tornado Alley, take note of what season it is. Or don't, because it doesn't matter: tornadoes can happen at any time of the year.

• Watch the skies. If they quickly become unusually dark, find shelter and tune in to a weather report. "Tornado watch" means that the conditions are ripe for a twister. Stay off the roads and stay glued to the weather. "Tornado warning" means that one has been spotted. Seek shelter immediately.

INSIDE JOB

• If the storm's a-brewin', find a safe, indoor spot. First choice: a storm shelter specifically designed to withstand tornadoes. They're usually underground and have strong, locking doors on top that won't get ripped off by a twister.

• Second choice: a basement. Hide under a heavy table to protect yourself from flying debris, and keep as far away as possible from any outside walls.

• No basement? Then find a room on the ground floor that doesn't touch any outside walls. A bathroom is best. Hide in the bathtub with a mattress over your head. Plumbing pipes are often buried in the ground, so a tub may be the only thing left where a house used to be. Wrap yourself in heavy blankets or quilts.

THE NOT-SO-GREAT OUTDOORS

• If you're outside, your biggest danger isn't the tornado—it's flying debris. Stay low. Find a ditch and lie facedown. Wind speeds around a tornado can reach upward of 200 mph, but at ground level (or below) they're usually much slower. Keep in mind: If there are heavy rains, be wary of flash floods.

• Don't hide in a car, which can be picked up and thrown, or under a highway overpass, which can leave you vulnerable to flying debris.

• An eerie calm can occur just before and after a tornado strikes, so don't think it's over just because the wind dies down. Danger remains until the sky is clear.

* * *

HOLD THE LIVER

Stranded and starving? Made a fresh kill? Don't chow down quite yet. The livers of many animals, including moose, walruses, and polar bears, contain toxic levels of vitamin A.

HOW TO COLLECT HONEY AND NOT GET STUNG TO DEATH

Honey is so packed with enzymes, immunity-boosting compounds, and quick energy that you'd be a fool not to stick your hand into the nearest beehive. Here's how to do it without getting stung hundreds of times.

WHAT YOU'LL NEED

- Container to store honey
- Fire-building materials
- Thick, light-colored protective clothing, (bees hate dark clothing)
- Thick gloves
- An axe
- A sharp knife
- Makeshift bee smoker, made from a sealable plastic container, a book, and a coffee can—or an empty water bottle
- Pine needles or dry leaves

HOW TO DO IT

1. Track down a beehive. That's not as simple as it sounds, because it's easy to mistake a wasp nest for a beehive, and wasp nests are notoriously free of honey and full of wasps. Wild honeybees build their homes out of beeswax, whereas wasps prefer to use mud or a pulpy substance made up of saliva and chewed-up wood. Honeybees are notoriously fussy and like to build their hives in a south-facing direction. They also sometimes set up shop in the crevices of trees. If you're still not quite sure if you've found a beehive, simply watch the insects come and go from their nest. If you spot bees coming and going, in all likelihood you've found a beehive.

2. The time of year can also be a factor in whether you'll be returning to your campsite with tons of delicious honey or barely enough to cover a single blackberry. Late summer is the ideal time of year to go looking for some. By then, the bees should have a large amount stored for the coming winter months.

3. Place pine needles or dry leaves in your "smoker." Set them on fire and wait until it's filled with smoke. Then slowly approach the hive and "smoke" the bees, fanning the smoke toward them. This simple trick should make them less likely to sting you.

4. For this step, you'll need to work as quickly as possible. Grab the axe and use it to make an opening in the side of the beehive. Then, swiftly reach inside and cut off a chunk of honeycomb with your knife. Don't confuse these "cells" with brood combs unless you want to go back to camp with a bunch of baby bees. Look for any area in the hive with capped cells that are light yellow or white. If you see brown ones, avoid them—they're probably brood combs.

5. As you do this, remain as calm as possible. Quick movements will only upset the bees further and increase the likelihood that they'll get their sting on. Toss one or more honeycombs in your empty container, slowly back away from the hive, and get out of there as quickly as possible.

6. When you're a safe distance away, use a twig or leaf to gently remove any bees still hanging around on your honeycombs. This should encourage them to fly back to their hive. Then check your clothing for stowaways and remove any stingers from your skin. (By the way, you shouldn't have attempted this if you're allergic to bee stings. We should have mentioned that from the get-go.)

7. Once back at your campsite, break up the honeycombs and strain them into a container (if you have a strainer). Or simply pop open the cells and do your best to get the honey into a container (or your mouth). Set aside the beeswax and store it as well; you can use it to coat and strengthen the string on a hunting bow, or melt it down into candles.

SURVIVAL MYTHS (AND TRUTHS)

Here are a few common bits of wilderness advice that are more fiction than fact. Don't trust the Old Wives!

Myth: Moss only grows on the north side of trees.

Fact: When it comes to providing directions, moss is a little green liar. While it tends to *prefer* to grow on the north side of trees, moss will actually wrap itself around just about any wooden surface provided it has enough moisture and doesn't receive too much direct sunlight. Also, the myth is especially not true if you're in the Southern Hemisphere. Down there, because of the position of the sun in the sky, moss prefers the *south* side of trees.

Myth: Poison ivy is contagious.

Fact: Nope! The unbearable itchy misery caused by this notorious plant is created by *urushiol*, an oily resin that can be found on its leaves, stems, and roots. If your skin comes into contact with the oil, you'll probably break out in a rash. However, unless you're totally covered in the stuff, you can't give someone else a rash by brushing up against him or her. If you have a nasty encounter with some poison ivy, change your clothes, wash off any exposed body parts, and prepare yourself for several days of uttering "Ugh, it itches like crazy!" when you're not reminding everyone around you that your rash isn't contagious.

Myth: If you can't find water, you can always drink your own urine.

Fact: If it's been a while since your last refreshing glass of water, your urine will be mostly comprising stuff you absolutely shouldn't put in your mouth. If you're fully hydrated, your pee is composed of around 95% water and 5% toxins that your body is trying to flush away. If you're dehydrated, the amount of toxins goes way, *way* up. So if you drink your urine while you're desperate for water, you're only going to put all of those nasty toxins back into your body. It also tastes really bad. (So we hear.)

37

Myth: You can lose most of your body heat from an exposed head.

Fact: While everybody from your mom to hard-sell haberdashers still repeats this one, it's complete hogwash. The myth has allegedly been traced back to a survival guide published in the 1950s by the U.S. Army. The author misinterpreted a study that observed a group of participants dressed in thick winter gear, but no hats. While you should definitely wear a hat if it's cold outside, that doesn't mean you can throw away your coat, gloves, and thermal underwear.

Myth: Eating snow is a great way to stay hydrated.

Fact: As it falls, snow absorbs air pollutants from cattle ranches, factories, and other sources. While the limited toxicity of snow still makes it safe enough to eat on occasion, you probably shouldn't stuff yourself with it, especially if you're desperate for water. Doing so may only dehydrate you further because your body will expend a substantial amount of energy melting and absorbing the snow.

HOW TO BUILD A SHELTER OUT OF ANIMAL POOP

Pioneers constructed temporary shelters out of sod and plugged in the gaps with cow chips. Here's how to do that...without the sod.

WHAT YOU'LL NEED

- Poop. You can purchase cow pies from a farm or ask a local zoo for their elephant manure.
- A big pot and a large outdoor grill
- Gloves
- A dust mask
- Bales of hay
- A screen frame
- A trowel
- A level
- A thick wooden board
- A ladder
- An 8 x 4 x 2-inch brick mold
- Plenty of mortar
- Materials to construct a roof and door

HOW TO DO IT

1. First, go fetch all the poop you'll need and pick a spot for your new cabin that's a goodly distance away from anyone with a normal sense of smell.

2. Once you've got everything in place, you'll begin by making all the poop bricks you'll need. Put on your gloves and start removing the non-fiber material from the doodie (undigested pebbles, leaves, etc.).

3. Next, grab your pot and fill it with poop and some water. Bring it all to a boil. Note: this procedure will help kill off all the bacteria. It will also create some unpleasant "poop steam," so you'll want to cover your face with a dust mask. Keep the pot simmering for four to six hours until you've got a substance that has the consistency of oatmeal.

4. Toss in some of the hay and mix it until you wind up with a thicker, stewlike substance. Pour it over the screen and drain off any remaining water. Fill your mold with some of the mix, smooth the top with the trowel, and

place your first brick aside to dry. Repeat this process until you've emptied the pot.

5. Repeat steps 3 and 4 until you have enough bricks to build your cabin. You'll need roughly 3,600 bricks for a 100-square-foot structure, so this could take a while.

6. Once you've got all your bricks, the rest of this project amounts to basic masonry. Get ready to build your first wall by creating a "footing," or a level surface. Grab the first brick, place it on the footing, put a bit of mortar on the side with the trowel, place the second brick next to it, and so on. Then add the second layer of bricks and use the level as you work to make sure everything's lining up correctly. Keep going until the wall is about 10 feet tall.

7. Once your first wall is in place, build the next three. (Once it's time to construct the fourth, you'll need to leave space for an entrance.) Once both sides of your wall reach the eight-foot mark, grab the board and place it on top of them. Then add several more rows of bricks over the board until the wall is lined up with the other three.

8. Construct the roof and a door. You won't be able to do this with bricks, so what you build them from depends on your available resources. You could use thatch or wood or, if you've found yourself in a nightmarish, postapocalyptic landscape, let your imagination run wild. Try out road signs, car doors, old IKEA furniture, or whatever you can find that might provide shelter from falling rain.

9. Once everything's in place, take a few steps back...because there's a good chance your new homestead will fall down. Hey, we're only here to tell you how to build a cabin out of poop, not a cabin made out of poop that will actually stand up against a strong breeze.

HOW TO
FIGHT FIRE

Our lawyers would probably appreciate it if we warned readers up front that fires are extremely dangerous and unpredictable. The most prudent action for all but the smallest of fires is to run away and allow professional firefighters to handle the situation.

THE FIRE TRIANGLE

There are three necessary components to any fire, sometimes called the "fire triangle": heat, fuel, and oxygen. To fight a fire, you will need to remove *at least one* of those elements—which one will depend on what kind of fire is burning and what tools you have available to best attack the fire triangle and stop the fire. Here are the most common—and effective—ways to fight a fire.

WATER

Water attacks every element of the fire. It cools down the surfaces, thereby reducing heat. If the fuel is something like wood, moistening it can make it less combustible. A steady flow of water can also deprive a fire of oxygen, thereby dousing the flames.

While most fires can be fought with water, there are some notable exceptions. Introducing water to an electrical fire doesn't really work, and it also introduces the risk of electrocution. Water also won't help you in an oil fire; because water and oil do not mix, spraying water on the fire will only cause the oil to splatter and the fire to spread.

FIRE EXTINGUISHER

While fire extinguishers look similar to each other, they vary in terms of what fire retardant they contain and what type of fire they are designed to fight. Some are simply pressurized water, while others contain things like carbon dioxide or dry chemicals. Be sure to take time to read the label on your extinguisher while the blaze is raging beside you. (Read fast, though.)

To use a fire extinguisher: First pull the pin (like a grenade!). Then aim at the *base* of the fire—not the dancing flames—and pull the lever or trigger. Continue spraying in a sweeping motion until the fire is out. Whether you are spraying pressurized water or some kind of chemical, you are trying to create a barrier between the fuel and the oxygen, thereby extinguishing the fire.

BLANKET

A commercially produced fire blanket is simply a large, fireproof cloth that can be used to smother small fires. Fire blankets can be made from a variety of materials, including Kevlar or chemically treated wool. (Older fire blankets were mostly made from fire-extinguishing-but-totally-poisonous asbestos, so if you have one of those lying around, you may want to replace it.)

Is it possible to smother a fire with a regular blanket? Maybe. The blanket may still separate the fuel from the oxygen and extinguish the fire. However, a blanket that is not fireproof could also become more fuel for the fire.

To use a fire blanket: Unfold it, and hold it in front of you like a shield. Approach the flames, using the blanket as a barrier, and then drape and release it onto the base of the fire. Once you've released the blanket, prance away shouting, "Holy moly, that was hot!"

FIREBREAK

In the event of a forest or grass fire, your only option may be to build a firebreak, ultimately and eventually removing the fuel from the fire.

Take note of what direction the fire is moving. You will want to build your break in that direction...and hope that the fire doesn't change course. Remove all of the vegetation, brush, etc., along a swath of ground in the path of the fire. Dig and overturn the topsoil to expose as much bare earth as possible. A bulldozer would be extremely useful, although you can also do this with a shovel.

If actually clearing the combustible material is not feasible, you may also be able to create a firebreak with water. Hose down the vegetation. This will make it less likely to combust, and may buy you enough time for the fire to put itself out. Make your firebreak as wide as possible. Especially in high winds, burning embers can carry a great distance, and even one could be enough to reignite on the other side of your break.

HOW TO NAVIGATE USING ONLY THE STARS

With smartphones and GPS, navigating the world has never been easier or more affordable (depending on your data plan). But if you ever find yourself without your phone, you can navigate using those little lights up in the sky, assuming they aren't obscured by smog or light pollution.

HOW TO DO IT

1. While most of the stars in the night sky will move, Polaris will always be above true north. (Perhaps *that's* why they call it the North Star.) To find it, first locate the constellation commonly called the Big Dipper. Imagine liquid pouring out of the ladle of the dipper, follow that trajectory, and you will find a very bright star. That's Polaris. (It's also located midway between the Big Dipper and the constellation Cassiopeia. Looking for the point between the two constellations can be easier when the Dipper is low in the sky.)

2. Now that you've identified true north, you can figure out all four cardinal directions. But you can also verify due east and west with the constellation Orion. The bright stars that form Orion's belt rise due east and set due west. So if it happens to be near the time they rise, you can also use them to orient you.

3. If you're pointed in the right direction, you should be able to get where you're going. But how far away is it? Would you believe you can calculate your latitude with Polaris?

The angle of Polaris in the sky corresponds exactly to your latitude. So if you're at the equator, Polaris will be on the horizon, and your latitude would be 0 degrees. At the North Pole, it will be directly overhead, and your latitude would be 90 degrees. Wherever you are, stand straight and hold your outstretched hand pointing toward Polaris. Estimate the angle of your arm and you've got your latitude.

4. Longitude is a bit trickier to calculate, but you can do it using the closest star of all: the sun. You'll need a watch set to Greenwich Mean Time, the time at longitude zero. If you're standing in Greenwich, England, when the sun hits its highest point in the sky, and then look down at your watch, you'll find it's exactly noon. Therefore, by noting Greenwich time when the sun hits its highest point wherever you are, you can calculate your longitude. One hour equates to 15 degrees of longitude, so if the sun hits its high point at 1:00 p.m., you are at 15 degrees longitude... likely in the middle of the Atlantic Ocean, and in dire need of help—such as a boat.

HOW TO POWER A SMARTPHONE WITH A FLASHLIGHT

Darkness falls, but you've got one of those fancy crank-powered "survival" flashlights. Now you can get a clear view of the wolves angling to rip you apart. What you really need is something to charge your cell phone so you can call for help.

WHAT YOU'LL NEED

- Cell phone
- 12-volt phone adapter
- Crank-powered flashlight
- Screwdrivers
- Voltage meter
- Soldering kit
- Wire cutter and stripper

HOW TO DO IT

1. Take your adapter cable and, with the wire cutters, snip off the end that plugs into your cigarette lighter.

2. Separate the two wires inside and strip about four inches of the protective coating. The positive, or "hot," wire is usually colored red; the black one is the ground wire. Set the cable aside.

3. Remove the screws from the flashlight casing and carefully crack it open.

4. Look for the generator wheel, near the butt end; just above it you'll see two lithium-ion cells—little "button" type batteries, like the kind that go in a wristwatch. Using your voltage meter, check the polarity on the battery contacts, identifying the positive and the ground.

5. Solder the corresponding adapter wires directly to the contacts on the button cells.

6. Cut a notch in the flashlight case to allow the cable to pass through, and close it all up.

7. Plug the cable into your cell phone, power it up, and document your successful project on Instagram.

HOW TO HACK POWER FROM A CAR BATTERY

As every child who has ever wanted to bring along a TV set on a camping trip knows, there's something fundamentally unfair about not being able to find an electrical outlet out in the wilderness. But you've got a strong source of electricity wheresoever you travel—namely, the car you're using to travel in the first place. Is it possible to power household appliances with your car's battery?

WHAT YOU'LL NEED

- DC-to-AC power inverter (see below)
- Terminal block
- Wire cutters
- Cable (the thickest and heaviest you can find)
- Red and black tape or marker pens
- Screwdriver
- Needle-nose pliers
- Cordless drill or another small electrical appliance

BEFORE YOU BEGIN

Batteries, including your car's, produce *direct current*, while your home electronics mostly work on *alternating current*. Devices built to work on one standard must be wired up to capacitors or oscillators in order to work properly on the other, and such a setup is beyond even the most determined do-it-yourselfer, especially in a survival situation. Going DC to DC, though—say, using your car battery to power a cordless drill—is eminently possible, if stupidly dangerous. We repeat—it's possible, but *very* stupid.

HOW TO DO IT

1. Open up your cordless drill and look for the power supply. Find the black ground wire and the red positive wire. Pull them out and replace them with the heavy electrical cables, crimping the ends in place with the needle-nosed pliers.

2. Attach the other ends of these wires to the terminal block—that is, an electrical connector that holds wires in place by

tightening screws. Make sure to keep your polarity straight.

3. Wire up the terminal block to the car battery—first connect the black ground, then the red positive terminal.

4. Turn on your drill, and hope that the mismatch in amperage doesn't burn it out or melt the insulation on your cable. In any case, if the cable gets uncomfortably warm, disconnect your rig immediately.

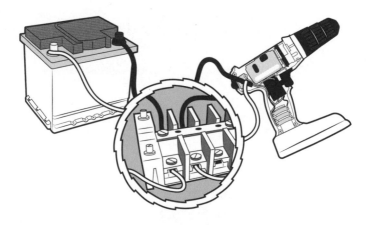

WILD PLANTS YOU CAN TOTALLY EAT

Being lost in the woods without a reliable food source is terrifying. In addition to the fear of starvation, there's also the fear of eating the wrong thing and poisoning yourself. Here, then, are some unexpected wild foods you can eat with confidence.

FIDDLEHEADS

Characteristics: The curled-up sprouts of young ferns, fiddleheads are found worldwide. The best-known varieties are the western sword fern, found along the Pacific coast, and the ostrich fern, common throughout New England and Canada. All varieties are packed with antioxidants and omega-3 fatty acids.

Preparation: Wash the fiddleheads in fresh water, then boil for 15 minutes, until tender crisp.

BURDOCK

Characteristics: The sticky burrs of this broad-leafed Old World plant were the inspiration for Velcro, and its taproot is a delicacy in Asian cuisine—it's pickled and served with sushi.

Preparation: Roots can be julienned and served raw for a sweet, mild crunch. A 10-minute soak in cold water draws out any lingering tannin bitterness. Wear gloves when handling the aboveground portions, though, as they produce a chemical that may cause skin irritation.

PINE NUTS

Characteristics: These rich, mild-flavored nuts are an essential ingredient for pesto. All pines produce pine nuts, but those from pinyon pines that grow in the southwestern U.S. and Mexico are the largest and sweetest. The best pine nuts come from well-watered trees that grow at elevations above 6,000 feet.

Preparation: In a survival situation, look for nuts under the scales of fallen pine cones. Remove the brown outer husks to reveal the pale nutmeats inside.

DANDELIONS

Characteristics: These ubiquitous lawn pests are a versatile food source. The buds and the broad leaves can both be eaten in salads. The leaves are an excellent source of vitamins A and C.

Preparation: They're bitter when raw, but a quick dunk in boiling water will make them more palatable. The thick taproot, which resembles a pale carrot in mature specimens, can be roasted, ground, and steeped to make a coffee substitute.

SAXIFRAGE

Characteristics: This ground-covering plant grows at high altitudes in cold temperatures, flourishing in areas as far north as the Canadian territory of Nunavut. There are many species of saxifrages, which typically grow as a circle of round, low-lying leaves surrounding a cluster of spindly stemmed flowers. The small blossoms have five petals and are usually white or pale yellow.

How to prepare: In Japan, the young succulent leaves are sometimes dipped in tempura batter and deep-fried...but they can also be eaten fresh.

HOW TO EAT INSECTS

Entomophagy is common throughout Asia and Africa, but it's a completely foreign concept in the Western world. However, because they are an efficient source of calories and protein, insects might be your last resort if you're lost and hungry...if you can find enough to make a meal...and pick the right ones to eat.

Ants. To get them to come out of an anthill, disturb the hill by poking it with a stick, and leave the stick there. Wait for ants to swarm it, then shake them off into a container. Don't put a lid on the container, though—ants secrete an acidic hormone when they feel threatened that imparts a bitter, vinegar-like flavor. Roast them right away. Their taste depends on the type of ant. Leaf-cutter ants are said to taste like popcorn when cooked, while lemon ants taste like, well, lemon.

Bees. If you dare seek out live bees to trap and eat, they are tasty and versatile. They can be roasted, or encased in butter and fried, which creates a "bee cookie." Bees do not taste like honey—they reportedly taste like bacon or sautéed mushrooms.

Waxworms. If you find a beehive and survive, look around for waxworms. They're a beehive parasite (a moth larvae) that are high in fatty acids and taste like pine nuts.

Dragonflies. Dip a reed in sugary sweet palm sap and wave it in the air. This will attract dragonflies, which will get stuck to the reed. Scrape off the bugs and boil them.

Crickets. Roasted crickets are a common street food in Southeast Asia and Mexico, but if you're somewhere less civilized that's loaded with crickets, here's how to catch them. Simply leave a jar on its side in a cricket-heavy area with some vegetative bait inside, such as an apple slice, a carrot, or some oats. Leave it overnight, and in the morning you'll have crickets. Remove the legs before you roast or pan-fry them, because they're stringy and tasteless.

Grasshoppers. These critters are high in calcium and protein. Generally they live in the same areas as crickets and can be harvested with similar traps.

Earthworms. They're commonly eaten raw in Venezuela, but they're a little better if you process them a bit first. Since they wiggle around in the dirt all day, worms are iron-rich, and their tiny cylindrical bodies are full of dirt. Gather the ones that have surfaced after a rainstorm (or look in holes that filled with water after a heavy rain), and soak them in water for three to four hours. (Alternately, you can gently squeeze the dirt out of them.) Dry them in the sun for a few hours, which mellows out the flavor and eliminates their innate sliminess. Fry until crispy.

Termites. Do like the monkeys do, and camp out over a termite nest, poke and twist a stick into it, pull it out, and eat the termites raw. Or, since you are not a monkey but (presumably) a human, put them in a jar to roast later.

Stinkbugs. Not only are they high in vitamin B, but they have a minor painkilling effect and taste a little like cinnamon. First, you have to get rid of their stink (to make them more palatable for eating). Soak them overnight in a jar, and then fry or roast them. A word of warning, however: cooking improves the taste and kills germs...but stinkbugs can and will survive the cooking process. Eating one marks one of the few opportunities for eating something that is both alive and cooked at the same time.

Hornworms. These creepy-crawlies are green and blend in with—and crawl around on and eat— tomato vines. They're easy to catch and are tasty when fried—oddly enough, they supposedly taste like fried green tomatoes.

Scorpions. While their nasty little stingers are not safe for consumption, the rest of a scorpion is...if you can handle their gritty texture. The best way to catch one? Find a scorpion hole, dig another hole a safe distance away, place a jar or cup inside, and check back the next day. Skewer it in the side with a sharp stick, wait for it to die, remove the tail, and roast it over an open fire.

Tarantulas. You can eat their heads, if you manage to catch one, but you may want to avoid their abdomens, which contain an icky brown goo that some people consider a delicacy. Their legs, meanwhile, supposedly taste like shrimp. Tarantulas can be enjoyed pan-fried, boiled, or grilled—but burn off the hair first.

WHAT *NOT* TO EAT

Brightly colored spots on bugs are generally a warning to predators—which in this case is you—that they are poisonous. Try to avoid bugs that bite or sting, ones that are already dead, or that are well known to carry or spread diseases. That means flies, ticks, and mosquitoes.

HOW TO EAT ROADKILL

Some things to consider if you get hungry when you're quite literally out on the road.

BEFORE YOU DINE

• An animal you hunt and kill doesn't taste much different from an animal somebody else killed with their truck. According to some insurance company estimates, about 1.2 million deer are hit by cars in the U.S. each year. That's a lot of free street meat!

• Roadkill meat is *de facto* "free range," organic, and free of hormones, chemicals, and preservatives.

• If you find an animal that's been struck and killed, it's generally fit to eat. If it's been flattened, it's too mangled and probably not worth your trouble.

• If the animal's eyes are clouded over, it's no longer fresh, but it's still edible...only just barely. Eat quickly.

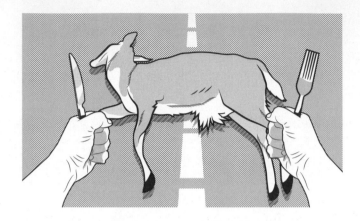

KEEP IT FRESH

• Of course, you want your roadkill to be as fresh as possible. If it's covered in maggots or flies, it's not freshly killed, and you wouldn't want it anyway with all those bugs involved.

• If the animal smells like it's rotting...it probably is. Avoid this roadkill.

• Rigor mortis isn't a deal-breaker—it sets in fast and doesn't imply that the animal isn't fresh.

SOME OTHER TIPS

• The main concern when eating roadkill is rabies. You're at greatest risk when handling the animal before slaughter. Always use rubber gloves when handling, gutting, and skinning roadkill. Rabies is cooked out, but ensure that you do it properly by boiling meat before cooking it. This is especially important for small, notorious rabies carriers such as raccoons, skunks, and foxes.

• Bear meat is not very tasty, but bear fat can be rendered to make cooking grease.

• The laws on roadkill vary widely from state to state. In West Virginia, dead animals are yours for the taking, provided you report it within 12 hours. In Alaska, the state government collects it all, butchers it, and uses it to feed needy families. It's fully legal to take what you find in Pennsylvania, Michigan, and Ohio, for example...and fully illegal in Texas, California, and Washington, where it's equated with poaching.

HOW TO TREAT YOUR FEET IN THE HEAT (AND IN THE COLD)

You should never discount the importance of feet. Whether you're marching into battle or trekking the wilderness, here's a complete strategy for protecting your trotters from extreme conditions.

WHAT YOU'LL NEED

In the Heat

- Well-fitting shoes
- Moisture-wicking socks
- Runner's tape
- Tincture of benzoin (friar's balsam)
- Alum
- Tannic acid
- Petroleum jelly
- Foot powder
- Water-repellent cream

In the Cold

- Thick socks made of wool or fleece
- High-quality boots
- Snow gaiters, or snow pants with attached gaiters
- Warm water
- Towels
- Cotton balls
- Bandages

HOW TO DO IT

1. **Check your equipment.** Your enemies are friction (which causes blisters) and moisture. Choose shoes or boots that are broken-in and snug but not tight, with a little wiggle room for the toes. Socks should be lightweight and sized appropriately. Favor moisture-wicking synthetic blends, and if you can, pack a fresh pair for every day you'll be on the move.

2. **Toughen up your tootsies.** Distance runners and Special Forces soldiers swear by a salve of tincture of benzoin (sold under the name friar's balsam), alum powder, and tannic acid in a petroleum jelly base. These active ingredients are the same chemicals used to tan leather. Applied to the feet over time, this mixture tones and strengthens the skin, making it resistant to blistering and injury...as if your feet were made of leather.

3. **Prevent hot spots.** Your toes move independently; prevent them from rubbing against each other by wrapping them with breathable runner's tape.

4. **Keep feet clean and dry.** Where possible, wash your feet every day. Don't soak; rinse with clean water and dry thoroughly, especially between the toes. Change socks often, and dust with foot powder to keep dry. Don't sleep in your socks if you can help it. During rest periods, let your bare feet get some fresh air—and let your shoes dry out, too. In prolonged wet conditions, rub in a water-repellent cream like Hydropel before you put on your socks.

5. **Treat blisters as soon as you notice them**. Clean the area with an alcohol swab. Drain by cutting a small slit with scissors— blisters lanced with a pin have a tendency to refill—leaving the skin as intact as possible. Clean, dry, and tape the area.

6. **Freezing weather presents special challenges.** Dry feet = happy feet. Wear the thickest socks that you can stuff into your boots when the temperature drifts toward the single digits. Grab a pair made out of IsoWool, fleece, or, if you don't mind a little scratchiness, good old-fashioned wool. As

for the boots themselves, find a pair that are rated appropriately for where you're headed. Any outdoor shop should be able to help you out with that. You may also want to invest in a pair of snow gaiters, which are wraps that go around your lower legs and will help prevent snow from slipping into your boots. Some types of snow pants even come with them attached.

7. **Did you ignore step #6?** Great, you've got frostbite. If you can, seek medical attention. If you can't, get indoors. Remove wet shoes and socks immediately and walk as little as possible...unless you want your toes to possibly snap off. Immerse your feet into warm water and wait for them to thaw. (This will hurt. A lot.) Afterward, dry your feet and place cotton balls or bandages between your toes to prevent rubbing. Finally, keep your feet elevated until you can receive proper medical care. If you absolutely must head back outdoors, make sure that your shoes and socks are dry.

HOW TO SURVIVE A PLANE CRASH

A few simple hints we hope will make a big impact.

- Listen to the flight attendant's preflight safety instructions, especially concerning emergency exits. You may think you've heard it all before, but different planes have different escape procedures.

- Many who survive the initial crash are killed by fire or fumes from burning upholstery because they hesitate or try to collect their belongings first. Leave your carry-on items behind and get off the plane immediately.

- Once you've escaped from the plane, get a safe distance away to protect yourself from an explosion, but stay close enough for rescuers to find you.

- If the plane crashes in water, don't inflate your life vest until you are safely out of the plane. An inflated life vest may get stuck in an exit or otherwise hamper your escape.

HOW TO SWING FROM A VINE

Swinging from vines may not be the most practical way to get around a tropical rainforest, but if it was good enough for Tarzan, it's good enough for you.

HOW TO DO IT

1. First, you'll need to climb a tree and find a vine. They should be plentiful if you're in a tropical rainforest; an estimated 90% of the world's vines are located in these lush environments. Lianas are the most common varieties, and they can grow to be up to a foot wide...and

3,000 feet long. They typically begin their life spans as tiny plants on the forest floor, but to reach the sunlight they crave, they wrap themselves around nearby trees. Once they reach daylight, they'll grow along treetops or back down toward the ground. Long story short, there should be plenty.

2. Once you've reached an appropriate height on your tree and have found a vine, you'll want to test it out. Give it a good tug and, with your feet on a firm branch, lift yourself up a bit. If it's not giving way, you should be good to go. Not to be a spoilsport, but finding a vine that's grown around enough limbs above your perch to be strong enough to support your weight could take a very long time.

3. If you're an inexperienced vine swinger, your first trip should be done a safe distance from the forest floor in case you fall. You'll want to try this a few times and get the hang of it before you attempt any jaunts from a height of 15 feet or more. If your vine is thin enough, you may want to tie some of the slack around your waist, for safety.

4. Ready for a real trip? Take a deep breath, grip the vine tightly, and jump off the limb. Once you're in the air, you'll want to immediately wrap your legs around the vine for further support.

5. Depending on the length of the vine and your surroundings, you should be able to travel anywhere from 10 to 40 yards at first. Needless to say, an area with a dense amount of trees isn't very practical for vine swinging. You'll also want to heed the oft-repeated suggestion from the *George of the Jungle* theme song: "Watch out for that tree!" Aim for a sturdy tree branch or return to your point of origin once you get bored.

6. Swinging from vine to vine might now seem like a totally awesome idea. In reality, this would be incredibly dangerous because you're not actually Tarzan. While your initial vine might be strong enough to support your weight, that doesn't mean that the next one you grab in mid-swing will be the same. This advanced level of vine swinging requires a substantial amount of skill, botanical knowledge, and luck.

THE BEASTS THAT WANT TO KILL YOU

"Know your enemy" is good advice, and that goes double for each of these fearsome animals.

GRAY WOLF

Where: Every continent except South America and Antarctica.

Specs: The largest males on record, discovered in Alaska, topped more than 120 pounds, and they can run at speeds exceeding 40 mph.

Hunting tactics: Gray wolves tend to hunt in packs of seven or eight and quietly stalk their prey before they go in for the kill. They'll pursue fleeing targets for over a mile, so don't attempt to escape a pack on foot because you can't outrun them (or at least not *all* of them). They also attack to the rear and sides of their prey. Once the prey is down, they'll tear into it with great ferocity.

Terrifying tidbits: Their jaws have a crushing pressure of 1,500 pounds per square inch. To help put that in perspective, the average German Shepherd's is a comparatively wimpy 740 pounds.

They also have voracious appetites. The average full-grown adult male can wolf down about 20 pounds of meat in one sitting.

GRIZZLY BEAR

Where: Western Canada, Wyoming, Montana, and Alaska.

Specs: They move at up to 35 mph and can weigh as much as 550 pounds.

Hunting tactics: Grizzly bears don't hunt in the traditional sense. They typically prefer to eat plants, and believe it or not, only about 10% of their diet consists of fish and meat. As for the latter, the "opportunistic omnivores" like to scavenge deer and elk corpses killed by harsh winter weather or other natural causes. But if threatened (and they're quite sensitive), they'll make a meal of you.

Terrifying tidbits: The average grizzly could crush a bowling ball with its teeth.

GREAT WHITE SHARK

Where: All coastal and offshore waters with a temperature range of 54–75°F.

Specs: Anywhere from 1,500 to 2,450 pounds, and they'll come at you at 35 mph.

Hunting tactics: As a general rule, great whites like to attack their prey from below. Those that roam areas off the east coast of North America like to hunt in shallow waters and are even known to use sand bars to ambush their targets.

Terrifying tidbits: Their sense of smell is extraordinary. Great whites can detect a single drop of blood in 25 gallons of water. They can sniff out a slightly larger amount from up to 3 miles away. On top of that, their light body color helps them easily blend in with coastal waters so you won't notice them creeping up on you until it's too late.

BENGAL TIGER

Where: India, Bangladesh, Bhutan, and Nepal.

Specs: They can run at 40 mph and weigh more than 500 pounds.

Hunting tactics: In the wild, these tigers prefer large game, typically Indian bison and chital and sambar deer. They approach their targets from behind or the side, and prefer quick kills. They go straight for the throat and drag their prey to a covered location before making a meal out of them.

Terrifying tidbits: Bengal tigers are among nature's most territorial animals. They aggressively scent-mark their territory, which can be as large as 38 square miles, and they aren't afraid of defending it with their razor-sharp retractable claws. These big kitties are also really loud. At night, their roars can be heard from over a mile away.

SALTWATER CROCODILE

Where: Southeast Asia and Australia.

Specs: 1,000 pounds of crocodile may pursue you at 18 mph in water, and 11 mph on land.

Hunting tactics: They like to lurk just below the surface of waterways. When a tasty target shows up, they burst out of the water, grab it, and drag it back under with them.

Terrifying tidbits: At 3,700 pounds per square inch, they have the strongest bite of any animal on the planet.

WHAT TO DO WITH YOUR POO

Leaving your waste lying around—literally—could pollute your water supply and/or attract large, scary animals. Like bears. Here are some ways to keep your surroundings both safe and sanitary.

YOU *CAN* TAKE IT WITH YOU

It's not the most pleasant option, but it's the one that's guaranteed to keep you and your campsite in good health. Both toilet paper and human feces take about a year to break down. And if they aren't buried properly, they can contaminate groundwater with *giardia,* a nasty intestinal parasite that causes explosive cases of diarrhea typically referred to as "beaver fever." Several national parks now have "pack it out" rules to encourage hikers in rural backcountry areas to clean up after themselves. Thankfully, this environmentally friendly procedure is pretty simple: Poop in a plastic bag or bucket, toss in the TP, and when you're heading back to civilization, take it all with you. Dispose of it properly when you find a trash can.

THE POOP BURRITO

A lot of backpackers swear by this technique. Lay a good amount of toilet paper on the ground, poop on it, and wrap it up, thus creating a "poop burrito." Then place the burrito in a plastic bag, and put the bag in a plastic container with a lid. This will help make getting it back to civilization easier and much less stinky. (Just make sure that the lid is sealed tightly.) We also recommend only using the container for this purpose and cleaning it thoroughly if you intend to use it again.

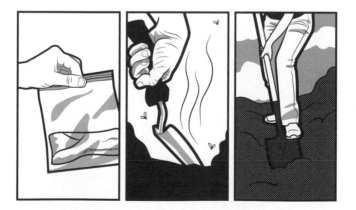

DIG A CATHOLE

Here's a method if you aren't planning to stick around for long and don't have any storage materials. Grab a small shovel (if you don't have a shovel, use your hands to dig) and find a location a safe distance from the nearest trail, the closest source of water, and your campsite. Dig a hole six to eight inches deep and roughly six inches wide. After you've done your business in the hole, cover it. Once you're all done, place a rock or another heavy object on top of the spot so you don't dig there again. To reduce the chances of contaminating groundwater, try to dig your catholes as far apart as possible and in sunny spots. Sunlight will help your waste decompose more quickly.

BUILD A LATRINE

If you'll be at your campsite for longer than a few nights, you may want to consider constructing a latrine. Using the tips outlined above for making a cathole, dig a deeper pit. How deep? That depends on how long you plan to stick around. A foot per week is one way to determine how low to go. To keep the smell under control and assist decomposition, cover your doodie with soil after every use. If you're the industrious type, you may want to consider building a makeshift commode to stick over the hole. Remove the bottom from a five-gallon bucket and place a toilet seat on top of it. If you don't have either of those, you could attempt to construct a wooden potty out of timber. Really bored or ambitious? Add a few walls, a door, and a roof to create your own wilderness outhouse.

THE SMEAR METHOD

It should go without saying that dropping your droppings off the edge of a cliff is considered very bad form—especially if there are climbers below. The frosty temperatures at high elevations means that poop decomposes slower; it can take years for the average mountaintop turd to completely break down. To avoid polluting the great outdoors, you may want to try the "smear method". Simply find a good-sized stone, do your dirty business, and smear the rock on yourself and then across the ground in much the same way you would ice a cake. Spreading it as thin as possible speeds up the decomposition process. (Sorry we ruined cake for you forever, though.)

WIPING IN THE WILDERNESS

Here's what to do when you have to drop a doo but don't know what to do...because you don't have any toilet paper.

WIPING IN THE WOODS

A forest is one of the easiest places on the planet to find natural TP. While pretty much every outdoor guide ever written will recommend using horsetails, there are plenty of other alternatives.

You could wipe with soft, non-rash-causing leaves, but those tend to tear at the worst possible moment. Still, the best leaf for the dirty job is the woolly lamb's ear. They're absorbent, not to mention as soft as, well, a lamb's ear. A smooth stick or a pine cone will also work, but clumps of grass or a few cattails will offer a much softer solution to the problem. Others swear by smooth river rocks and old man's beard, a type of pale greenish-gray lichen that grows on lots of different trees.

WIPING ON A MOUNTAINTOP

If you're scaling a mighty big peak and have to take a mighty big dump above the timberline, tracking down natural TP is going to be mighty big concern. If you can't find a smooth stone or suitable vegetation, snow can work. Grab a clump, squeeze it into the shape of a thin cone, and start wiping. (As a bonus, sticking ice-cold materials in  such a sensitive place will also eliminate any sort of drowsiness whatsoever.) However, this trick won't work well if the snow is too powdery or dry.

WIPING WITH WATER

If all else fails or if you've found yourself in a region (such as a desert) where natural TP is sparse, there's always what we'll call "the rinsing

method." Unfortunately, this will require you to have two bars of soap and at least a liter of water that you don't need for any other purpose. First, designate your left arm as "the water arm" and your right arm as "the cleaning arm." Then squat and go poo. Afterward, grab your right butt cheek with your left hand. Then grab the water bottle and pour some water down your left arm. The force of gravity and various laws of physics will send the water sliding down your arm to the right spot. Next, scrub away with the soap. Then pour more water down your arm. That should wash away the soap. When things finally feel clean down there, stand up and rinse off your bar of soap. Once you're all done, clean your hands with more water and that second bar of soap (for obvious reasons).

As with the rolls that you can buy in a store, be sure to dispose of your makeshift wiping material by properly burying it once you're all done. Give a hoot! Don't poo-lute! (And be sure to wash your hands afterward, if possible.)

MAKE YOUR PEE WORK FOR YOU

Even if you're stuck in the wilderness, what's the one thing you'll never be without? Your own urine. Here are some very useful things you can do with what you've been wrongly calling "waste."

Gas mask. Soldiers in World War I found that during mustard gas attacks by German soldiers, they could resist the poisonous fumes if they breathed through urine-soaked rags they held over their faces.

Mouthwash. Urine has ammonia in it, and that kills a lot of bacteria. Do as the Romans did, and gargle with pee, which is even said to whiten teeth.

Anesthetic. We really hope you never lose a limb, a digit, or a nose, but if you do, put a little pee on it. Since the 1500s, battlefield doctors have occasionally used more-sterile-than-stagnant-water urine to clean wounds or exposed spots where body parts used to be.

HOW TO GET OUT
OF A DEEP HOLE

*We're got going to ask how you fell into the hole.
Let's focus on how to get you out of the hole.*

How deep is less important than how steep.
Any hole with less than a sheer drop is essentially
a hill. That includes virtually all natural holes,
and it's worth taking a quick look at the physics of
granular solids to understand why.

When you dig a hole at the beach, you'll notice
that you can't dig the sides straight down; the sand
rushes in to fill the bottom of the hole. When you
barbecue, notice that no matter how carefully
you stack your charcoal briquets, the pile always
starts to spread. In both cases, you're observing
the "angle of repose" in action. This is the natural
slope that granular materials will seek when you
pile them up or dig into them. Different substances
have different angles of repose, and conditions of
moisture or compression will affect a material's
capacity to hold an angle. Wet sand, for instance,
will hold a 45-degree angle; dry sand's angle of
repose is 30 degrees.

In practical terms, the critical angle for most materials, even moist packed earth, is less than 45 degrees—which means that the slope of most naturally occurring holes or unreinforced pit traps will be gradual enough for you to scramble out. Stay low to the slope, using both your arms and your legs to move. If the slope starts to shear away, that's good; that's the earth seeking its angle of repose. Push the loose material behind you, filling in the bottom of the pit, and keep moving upward.

A vertical manmade hole—say, a well or a tiger trap—will make climbing more difficult. But such a hole must of necessity be reinforced, as by stone blocks or timbers. Here's how to get out:

Flatten yourself against the wall and search for finger- and toeholds in between the stones or beams, hoisting yourself upward bit by bit. If the well is both relatively smooth and very narrow— that is, if you cannot sit down with your legs stretched straight—use your back for additional leverage. Position your feet against the far wall. Press against the near wall with your hands and your backside, and push straight up a foot or so at a time.

HOW TO CAMP ON THE SIDE OF A CLIFF

Why might you be forced to do this someday? For one thing, most hungry predators are incapable of scaling cliffs. They're a safe place to get some shut-eye (so long as you don't fall off, that is).

HOW TO DO IT

1. If you're lucky, all the lions and tigers and bears that might be hot on your heels will give you enough time to gather the supplies you'll need. First, find some fibrous plants that will make good rope. Dogbane and milkweed are plentiful in many North American forests, and they're great for this sort of thing. Look for stalks that are brown and tall.

2. Strip off the outer bark and take out the fibrous interior of the plant. Remove any little bits of wood and fasten it all together. You'll need at least 40 feet of rope.

3. You'll also need a makeshift hammock. If you've got enough freshly made rope lying around—and plenty of time on your hands— you could try making one. An animal skin is a quicker and, perhaps, more practical alternative. Track down an elk, deer, or another animal large enough to make a good hammock. Kill it, skin it, and remove all the tissue and fat. Ideally, you would then stretch, salt, and dry the skin (a process that usually takes several weeks). You probably don't have that kind of time, though. If you're feeling particularly cocky, ambitious, and/or bored, you could try using the skins to construct a portaledge. These hangable tents are more comfortable than hammocks. Cliff climbers love them, and they'll keep the rain off your head.

4. Because you're not properly drying the animal skin, you'll want to double or even triple the layers in your hammock. Using a sharp object, poke two holes in either side of your new (and likely very smelly) hammock and attach two lengths of rope to them. If you've constructed a portaledge, do the same with it.

5. You'll also need bolts or spikes that will secure your hammock/portaledge to the cliff. Ideally, you'd have a few bolt anchors at your disposal. Forge some sturdy spikes, and while you're at it, make a hammer and a carabiner. You'll need at least eight spikes.

6. If you're beginning to think that this is an extraordinarily stupid idea, well, you're probably right about that. Nevertheless, find yourself a cliff and create a makeshift harness for yourself out of the rope. Cut the remainder into four or more strips. Sling them over your shoulder along with the hammock/portaledge. Step into the harness and connect the carabiner to it.

7. Pound a spike into the rock face and attach the first strip of rope to it and the other side to your carabiner. Start climbing. If you run into trouble, the rope *should* prevent you from falling all the way down to the bottom of the cliff. Pound a second spike into the rock face, tie the next line of rope to your carabiner, and remove the first one. Repeat this process until you're high enough to avoid the reach

of predators and/or find a lovely view of the landscape below.

8. Drive two more spikes into the rock face and connect the rope from the hammock/portaledge to each. Drive a third spike into the cliff and connect another line of rope to it and your carabiner (safety first!). Climb inside and get ready for what could turn into a wild night. While you may be a safe distance from all those lions, tigers, and bears, that doesn't mean that the howling wind up here won't keep you awake all night. Or that a boulder won't come tumbling down the cliff and knock you into oblivion. Or that you won't be attacked by eagles. Sweet dreams!

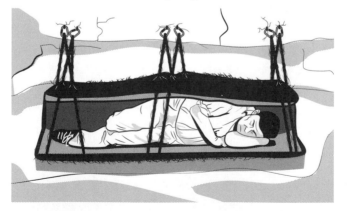

HOW TO FIND (AND DRY OUT) FIREWOOD

First you've got to find wood you can burn, and then you've got to dry it out so you can burn it.
It's a whole thing.

• Most of the twigs and branches you'll find on the ground won't be of much use right away. This is because they're like sponges when it comes to rain, fog, dew, etc., making them too "green" for burning. Dead wood sucks up moisture, whereas dead limbs from standing trees make great fuel.

• As you continue your search, look for trees in sunny areas. It should go without saying that their branches won't be as wet as those from trees in denser regions. A failsafe trick to determine whether a branch or twig should be collected: Break it in half. If it makes a snapping noise and it's easy to break, then it's worth hauling back to your campsite.

• If you've found enough dry firewood to build and keep a fire going for a while, well, congratulations, but that doesn't mean that a rainstorm isn't just around the corner. For one reason or another, you may find yourself forced to dry out wood at some point. In normal circumstances, it can take anywhere from six to eight months for green firewood to "season" and be dry enough for burning. Obviously, you don't have that kind of time if you're shivering in the wilderness.

• First things first: Do your best to keep your firewood away from the ground, which is wet. Store it on an elevated surface in a dry place. This could be a makeshift woodshed, if you've got the time and resources to build one, or whatever you're using for shelter. Just be sure to check the wood for termites and other creepy crawlies if you plan on sleeping next to it.

• Once you've found (or built) a dry place to store your firewood, place it in stacks no taller than four feet high. Make sure there's plenty of room between the pieces to allow for air to circulate and moisture to evaporate. Don't cover the wood with a tarp or anything like that. This will only help seal in the moisture and keep the wood wet.

• During your time in the wilderness, you should keep your firewood stash well stocked and your driest pieces all in the same place. If you absolutely, positively need to get a fire going and don't have any dry firewood available, you could try whittling away the exterior bark of the driest pieces. The interior may be dry enough to burn. Once you get the fire going, you can add the wetter wood, but do so slowly, one piece at a time. Too much wet wood could kill the flames. Placing wetter pieces next to the fire will help them dry out, but don't expect any miracles. Also, the wetter the wood, the greater the amount of smoke it will produce. Keep that in mind if you're building a fire in a poorly ventilated cave.

• Some additional tips: Avoid oak trees. Their wood takes an unusually long time to season. The larger the piece of wood, the longer it will take to dry out, which is why you'll want to fill your firewood stash with thin branches instead of huge logs.

HOW TO SURVIVE A SNAKEBITE

They're lovable, they're huggable, they're...neither of those things. What's wrong with you? Uh oh. Did you get too friendly with a venomous snake and it bit you? Here's how to survive the ordeal.

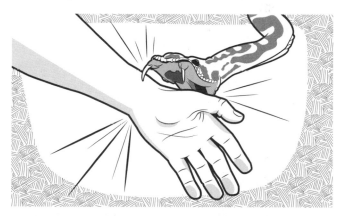

DON'T SUCK OUT THE POISON

You've probably seen this method used in old Westerns, or *Caddyshack II*. The thing is, it doesn't really work—it could actually make things worse. Sucking on a bite could infect the wound, or damage nerves and blood vessels adjacent to the bite site. Plus, the time you spend treating the bite like it's a Slurpee constitutes valuable minutes that would be better spent seeking medical attention.

DON'T MAKE A TOURNIQUET

Wilderness survival books once claimed that a tourniquet could help cut off circulation in the area surrounding a snakebite, preventing the venom from circulating and thereby allowing the victim enough time to find a doctor. However, several studies in recent years have determined that they're ineffective in most cases. Furthermore, a tourniquet could cut off circulation entirely. That means you could wind up with a nasty case of gangrene that might require you to have a limb amputated.

DON'T DIP

Dipping the bite in either warm water or sour milk—both old folk remedies—won't work. It's been theorized that both of these liquids had a spongelike effect on venom. Nope!

HERE'S WHAT YOU *SHOULD* DO:

• Remain calm. Freaking out, running around in circles, raising your fists to the sky, and that sort of thing? These actions will not help you. Also: Get away from the snake if it's still hanging around, especially if it looks grumpy.

• Was the snake that bit you actually venomous? Some common species of dangerous snakes in North America include: rattlesnakes, copperheads, water moccasins, and coral snakes. If you can't identify the reptile that sunk its fangs into you, see if you develop any common symptoms of a poisonous bite. (The waiting is the hardest part.) They'll develop within 20 to 60 minutes and could include: chills, fever, weakness, nausea, blurred vision, and/or breathing difficulties. Don't wait to head back to civilization if you're unsure. Get moving as soon as you can. You'll need medical attention as quickly as possible if the snake's bite was, indeed, poisonous.

• Do your best not to move an arm or leg if you've been bitten on one of these limbs. Keep it as still as possible using a splint. The more you move the bitten body part, the more likely it is that the venom will spread through your bloodstream. Keep the bite below the level of your heart if you can. This should help minimize the possibility of the venom reaching your vital organs. If you've been bitten on a leg, this will obviously make getting to a doctor an unpleasant ordeal. If you're traveling with companions, have them help you keep moving while keeping the leg as still as you can.

• Remove any jewelry or tight clothing if you've been bitten on a limb. This includes watches, shoes, and bracelets. The increased pressure on the limb may cause it to swell, which is anything but.

• Don't drink any alcohol or water. Alcohol is an especially bad idea. It will speed up the absorption of the venom in your system.

• Don't eat anything either.

• Again, seek medical attention as soon as possible. That's all there is to it. If you've been bitten by a poisonous snake in the wild, nothing within your power or immediate surroundings is likely to help.

The nearest hospital should have an appropriate antivenom on hand that will help you survive the bite.

• If you're an expert on snakes and know for a fact that you haven't been bitten by a poisonous one, that doesn't mean that you shouldn't consult a doctor as soon as you can. The bite could become infected and might cause any number of problems, especially if you don't have any bandages or medical supplies lying around.

* * *

HOW TO MAKE A RABBIT STICK

This ancient weapon (also called a throwing stick) is a precursor to the boomerang. It won't come flying back to you after you toss it, but it will help you hunt small animals like squirrels and rabbits. Whittle a chunk of solid wood, preferably oak, until it's flat on the top, bottom, and edges, and has a 45-degree angle in the middle. Now, point your rabbit stick at your target with your nondominant arm, raise and lower the stick to build momentum, and release when it's parallel to your other arm. If all goes as planned, it should zip off to your target.

HOW TO MAKE JERKY IN THE WILD

What's portable, has an indefinite expiration date, and is totally delicious? Jerky, every outdoorsman's second- or third- or fourth- or sometimes fifth-favorite snack!

WHAT YOU'LL NEED

- Meat. Just about anything should work. We suggest using cutlets from a deer, rabbit, squirrel, or bear...if you've managed to fight one and win, of course. (See page 104.)
- Three tree branches
- Three sticks
- Twine
- Everything you'll need to build a small campfire
- A knife, containers, and other cooking utensils
- Salt
- Water

HOW TO DO IT

1. Take the three tree branches and arrange them into the shape of a teepee. This will serve as a tripod that will help you dehydrate your jerky. Then grab the three other sticks and tie them to the base of the tripod toward the top. Now you've got the drying racks.

2. Wait until the late morning of a sunny day (this will be important later on). Using the knife, trim away the fat from each bit of meat. Slice "against the grain" of each piece as you cut it into thin strips between $1/4$ and $1/8$ of an inch thick.

3. Now it's time to whip together the "marinade" that will serve as your salt cure. Grab a pot and, based on which ingredients you have available, mix up a marinade. Place the meat slices in the pot and cover it. Keep an eye on it while you work on the next step. If you're making grizzly jerky, there's a good chance the smell might attract some of its still-living, and possibly very vengeful, bear friends. Typically, you'd want to let the meat sit in the marinade overnight, but it could go bad

without refrigeration, so that isn't an option out here.

4. Build a small campfire and allow it to burn down to the embers. Once you've got a good-sized bed of hot coals, place the tripod over them and arrange the slices of meat on the drying racks.

5. Make sure that the meat strips aren't touching one another. You'll want to maximize their exposure to air and to the coals' heat and smoke, in addition to direct sunlight, which will be doing most of the work. The smoke should prevent any pesky insects from setting up shop in the meat, but be sure to shoo away any flies or other bugs. Disgusting maggots will put the "jerk" in your jerky, and you don't want that.

6. Remember: The goal here isn't to cook the meat. If those slices start sizzling, remove some of the coals.

7. After several hours, the meat should be dry enough to discourage bugs from going after it. Move the tripod to keep it in direct sunlight

if needed. Check each slice to see if it's dry as sunset approaches. If they're good to go, congrats, you're a huge jerk! (By which we mean you've just made jerky.)

8. If the meat is still wet, place the strips in an enclosed container where animals can't get to them. Say a quick prayer for good weather and repeat steps 4 and 5 until the strips are dry the following day.

9. Store your jerky in a cool, dry place. It won't taste as good as the stuff you can buy at the truck stop, but it should keep you going if you wind up on a long march back to civilization. If stored correctly, the jerky should remain safe to eat for at least a few weeks.

* * *

LONGEST TIME ADRIFT AT SEA

Captain Oguri Jukichi and sailor Otokichi were off the Japanese coast in October 1813 when their ship was disabled in a storm. They floated all the way across the Pacific and were rescued off the California coast on March 24, 1815. Total time at sea: 484 days.

HOW TO FIGHT A BEAR AND WIN

If you ask five burly fellows how to fight a bear, you're going to get five different answers. Still, there are specific strategies that you should be aware of in the event that you go toe-to-toe with a bear. (The most effective strategy may vary by situation and by bear.)

LEARN

Bears are nature's college students: they'll eat anything, and they have no shame in scavenging. When they wander into a campsite, they generally aren't looking to rumble—they're hoping to find a backpack full of Clif Bars. Many bears will be just as eager to avoid you as you are to avoid them. That said, like college students, some bears are just jerks.

PREVENT

There's probably an old proverb that says the easiest way to win a bear fight is not to fight at all. To keep a bear from taking interest in your campsite, store all food, food waste, deodorant—anything that a bear might sniff and take interest in—inside a locked "bear canister." Then stash these purpose-built containers at least 100 feet outside of your camp while you're away. When you're at your campsite, a fire will keep most bears away.

ESCAPE

If you're confronted by a bear, your first move should be to get away. Most experts say not to run, because this can trigger a bear's predator instinct. Instead, walk with a purpose in another direction, avoiding eye contact. Often, the bear will do the same, and you'll be like coworkers who bumped into each other in an adult bookstore. If you do run, going up or down a hill in a zigzag pattern will be more challenging for the bear, given its body weight and short legs. Even so, you are very unlikely to outrun a bear.

FRIGHTEN

Believe it or not, a little peacocking can convince a bear not to mess with you. Stand tall, with your arms up, or if you're wearing a jacket, hold your jacket open to make yourself look as big as possible. Growl, shout, and bang pots and pans if you've got them. You're going to look ridiculous, but the bear is calculating whether you're worth the effort of a fight—the more intimidating you can look, the more likely it is that the bear will decide not to bother.

FIGHT!

If you were unable to get away and the bear was not discouraged by your growly face, it's time to tango. If you're lucky enough to have a gun, now's the time to start shooting. Aim for the lower neck and chest, and keep firing—it will take more than one bullet to bring down a 1,400-pound Kodiak. If you have a knife, direct your stabbing toward the bear's neck. Spraying the charging beast with Bear Mace is also an option, though some experts say this only makes the bear angrier—and let's be honest, it's not the most manly approach.

Assuming you came into this confrontation unarmed, you need to arm yourself in a hurry. Grab a branch or heavy rock if you can. Aim for the bear's weak spots: the eyes, snout, and neck. If the bear is a boy, a kick to the nuts is also an option. If you manage to stun the bear enough that it momentarily backs off, try to get away.

Killing the bear with your bare hands will be a tall order, but if you put up enough of a fight, you may convince him to simply shake hands and go your separate ways. (Metaphorically speaking. Do not try to shake hands with a bear.)

MEDICAL SOLUTIONS IN A PINCH

Because nobody ever remembers to bring a first-aid kit, here are some quick fixes with common items.

CUTS

• Large, shallow cuts or scrapes can be covered with an improvised bandage made out of a sanitary napkin and duct tape.

• Superglue can be used to seal the edges of a cut. Only try this on wounds two inches long or smaller, and clean the affected area carefully with soap and water beforehand.

• The membrane from the inside of an eggshell makes a natural bandage for small scrapes.

• Stanch a nosebleed with a tampon.

• Tea tree essential oil and coconut oil both have antibacterial and antifungal properties, making them a good basis for an improvised antibiotic ointment.

STINGS AND RASHES

• Relieve the itch of mosquito bites by applying roll-on deodorant to the affected area.

• Treat bee or wasp stings with a paste of meat tenderizer and water. The papaya enzymes in the tenderizer break down the toxic proteins in the insect venom.

• Raw onion is also effective on insect stings. Apply a whole slice, or blend to a paste and dress with gauze.

• The phytochemicals in colloidal oatmeal will soothe the itchy, inflamed skin brought on by conditions like eczema or hives. Pulverize rolled oats to powder in your food processor, and add to a warm bath.

BURNS

• Witch hazel is an effective treatment for skin damage due to sunburn.

• To dress minor burns, smear with honey and wrap in clean gauze. The honey keeps the dressing moist and prevents infection, and the nutrients promote skin regrowth.

IMPACT INJURIES

• Need an ice pack for a bruise? Just grab a bag of frozen peas.

• A poultice of raw potato can bring down swelling. Grate the potato to mush and slather on the affected area; wrap in plastic wrap to keep in place and leave it on for an hour.

• Applying toothpaste to a bruise before bed is reputed to help it fade overnight.

TUMMY TROUBLES

• Poison treatments may call for induced vomiting. A one-to-one solution of mustard and water can get the job done as effectively as syrup of ipecac, and is less risky than a finger down the throat.

• For a burning mouth from eating hot chilies, mix a half-teaspoon of baking soda into a glass of water; swish and spit, then rinse your mouth with plain water.

HOW TO SURVIVE ADRIFT AT SEA

Chinese merchant seaman Poon Lim had his ship sunk by torpedoes during World War II. The lone survivor of the attack, he drifted on an eight-foot raft for 133 days before being rescued—the longest time on record. Lim's ingenuity and courage were an inspiration to the British navy, who used his ordeal as the basis for their survival training. Here are some lessons they took from Poon Lim's ordeal.

TAKE STOCK

Lifeboats typically come equipped with a small supply of drinking water, nonperishable food, a first-aid kit, and a signaling device. Assume that rescue will come later rather than sooner, and ration your supplies from the start. This will buy you time to find alternate sources for food and water before you reach a crisis.

USE WHAT YOU HAVE

When your resources are stripped to the bare
essentials, use them to the fullest. Poon Lim
stripped his life jacket's canvas cover to block
the sun and catch rainwater. A flashlight spring
became a fishing hook, and a flattened biscuit tin
became a crude knife.

ATTEND TO YOUR NEEDS

You can last weeks without food, but thirst kills
within days. If you can steer your craft, head
downwind to find rain; rig a tarp out of a life jacket
to catch it. There are other options, too: At several
points, Lim resorted to drinking fish blood.

STAY ACTIVE

Nothing is more lethal than losing the will to live. Routine and activity can help to keep despair at bay. Even though he was a poor swimmer, Poon Lim took laps around his raft every day he could, tying a lifeline around his waist for safety. If there's a logbook among your supplies, keep a journal. Give yourself a reason to look forward to every tomorrow, even if you're drifting in a lifeboat in the middle of the ocean.

GET RESCUED

If you spot a ship or plane while on the open water, use a flare if you still have one, or flash SOS with a flashlight or by reflecting sunlight with a mirror or other shiny surface. Be alert to signs of land nearby: changes in water color, stationary clouds, and an increase in birds. If you must come to harbor on your own, your greatest danger is capsizing. Add weight to the bottom of your craft to make it more stable; on your final approach to shore, fill the hull with water.

HOW TO ESCAPE HUNGRY SHARKS

Shark attacks on humans are rare overall, resulting in just four annual deaths worldwide. But when they do occur, it's in open water. If you're a swimmer or a surfer, here's how to keep safe.

STAY AWAY

If you want to avoid sharks, don't go where the sharks go—and sharks go where the food is. Keep clear of large schools of fish, seals, or sea lions. Sharks prefer live prey to offal, but they will eat

the trash fish and seabirds that congregate around chum and garbage. For this reason, avoid the wake of fishing vessels. Sharks like bounded areas that keep prey contained, like channels, harbor entrances, and steep drop-offs. Like all hunters, sharks know the value of camouflage, preferring murky waters to clear. Many species congregate near river mouths after heavy rain, when sewer runoff and carrion wash out to sea and attract fish.

AVOID DETECTION

Sharks don't have great eyesight, but they can see contrast pretty well and are attracted by movement. Avoid wearing bright colors—yellow and orange—or glittery jewelry, which can be mistaken for fish scales. That old story about sharks being attracted to menstruating women sounds like a sexist myth, but a shark really can smell even small amounts of blood in the water from up to a mile away—if you get a cut or scrape, you should get out of the water right away.

If possible, always swim with a buddy. Sharks will plow through a shoal of small fish, but with larger prey, they prefer to pick off stragglers.

MIND THE FISH

If you see a shark approaching, remain calm—
but prepare for action. He may not have even
noticed you, and if you don't splash, he might not.
Stay as still as you can, treading water. Watch
his approach pattern. If he's coming straight on,
chances are he's just curious; most likely he'll
give you a bump with his nose and move on. If he
zigzags or circles, though, he's searching for an
angle of attack.

DEFEND YOURSELF

Protect your blind spots, if you can; get your back
against a boat or pier, or go back-to-back with
your swimming buddy. Conventional wisdom
holds that you can drive off a shark with a sock to
the nose, but it's hard to wind up for a good punch
underwater. Jabbing and clawing at the eyes or
gills will be more effective. If he gets you in his
jaws, don't play dead—fight harder. Get him a good
one in the eye, and that shark will remember why
he so rarely attacks humans: We're more trouble
than we're worth.

HOW TO BOOST YOUR PHONE SIGNAL

The worst part of getting stuck in the middle of nowhere—worse than starving to death or getting eaten by bears—is that it's so booooorrrring. Good thing you brought that smartphone...but oh no, no bars! Here's how to get a decent cell signal out in the wild so you can get on Twitter. Or contact the authorities, we suppose.

HOW TO DO IT

• Since you've apparently got a power source to refuel your phone (like one of those nifty wind-up chargers), you could also make use of a signal booster. Just plug it in, raise the antenna, and let it do its thing. There are also battery-powered products on the market, like the Outdoor Ranger, that promise to "boost your bars." They're popular among backpackers and can help improve a phone's signal when it's many miles from the nearest cell tower. Emergency rescue crews and rural research teams also rely on spendy satellite Wi-Fi antennas. But you probably didn't bring

117

any of that stuff with you when you got lost in the woods, did you?

• Some crafty backpackers swear by "cantennas." These makeshift boosters are typically made out of tin cans, but Pringles containers seem to work best—probably because they're very tall cans and coated with metallic paper. A cantenna won't help you make a phone call (unless you use an Internet-based phone service like Skype), but one could enable you to surf the web several miles from civilization. Building one involves cleaning out the can, pounding holes in the side, and running a few wires into it. We suggest Googling "Pringles can antenna" and printing out the directions *before* you hit the trail.

• If you didn't pack any wires or Pringles, you'll have to go looking for a signal the old-fashioned way. Being a ways from the nearest cell tower isn't going to do you any favors. All the geographical obstructions in your way won't either. If you've found yourself in a hilly region with lots of trees, get yourself to the highest point possible. If that involves climbing a tree, go for it—but remember, safety first! If there's a mountain blocking the tower, we've got two words for you: start hiking.

• If you'd rather try a MacGyver-style trick, break out a paper clip. Unbend the paper clip until it's in a straight line, and stick one end of it into the internal antenna hole on your phone. Then bend the paper clip until it lies flat against the back of your phone. Secure the clip with Scotch tape, gum, or whatever other adhesive you have at your disposal. With any luck, it should boost your reception by a bar or more.

* * *

FIGHT AN UNARMED STREET TOUGH

• Bunch your keys in your hand with the ends sticking out between your fingers. A strike to the neck, eye, or groin could end the attack right away.

• Kick for the groin. It will give you a longer reach than your assailant.

• Other weapons: comb (drag it underneath the nose); umbrella (for puncturing); makeup (blow powder in the assailant's face to blind him); also nail files, pens, or anything with a point.

TRUE TALES OF WEIRD SURVIVAL: MAURO PROSPERI

SUPER MAURO

Italian policeman Mauro Prosperi spends his off days participating in marathons and even more grueling races. In 1994, he and his cousin signed up for the Marathon des Sables ("Marathon of the Sands"), one of the most intense events of its kind on the planet. The event sends participants racing through the Sahara Desert in southern Morocco in temperatures exceeding 104°F. It's so dangerous that organizers ask participants where they would like to have their bodies sent if they die during the race.

Four days into race, Prosperi encountered a sudden sandstorm. Rather than stop, he stubbornly kept running, eager to stay in fourth place and, with any luck, catch up with the runners ahead of him. When the storm ended six hours later, he was completely off course and totally lost.

BLOOD AND GUTS

Prosperi spent the next 36 hours wandering the desert. After depleting all his water and food supplies, he found an abandoned Muslim shrine and stuck a small Italian flag he had brought with him on the roof, hoping that it might attract a rescue plane. Undaunted by the corpse of a holy man inside, he used it for shelter and caught and ate the bats that were living on the ceiling. As he later told reporters, "I decided to drink their blood. I grabbed a handful of bats, cut their heads and mushed up their insides with a knife, then sucked them out. I ate at least 20 of them, raw. I only did what they do to their prey."

Fearing the worst after three days at the shrine, Prosperi attempted suicide with a pen knife, but his own thickened blood caused the wounds to clot. He regained his composure and struggled onward while using a compass and the passing clouds overhead as guides. Along the way, he made meals out of insects, lizards, and cactuses. For water, he sipped dew off whatever plants he could find. On the eighth day of his journey, he stumbled upon an oasis, and the next afternoon, a group of goat herders.

KEEP GOING

By then, Prosperi had wandered roughly 186 miles off course and into neighboring Algeria. He also lost nearly 40 pounds during his ordeal. For months afterward, his body would only allow him to absorb liquids. It took him nearly two years to fully recover from his unfortunate mishap.

Unswayed by his terrifying experiences, Prosperi signed up for the 1996 Marathon des Sables. Organizers rejected him, although he was accepted in 1998. That year, he had to quit mid-race...because of a stubbed toe of all things. He finally ran the entirety of the desert race in 2012.

NATURAL MEDICINES FOUND IN THE WILD

Today's fancy scientists still derive cures from ancient sources. Ethnobotanists track down the plants that traditional societies still use as curatives and isolate the chemical compounds that give them their effect. Here are some natural cures you might find in the wilderness around you.

Calendula. Sometimes called "pot marigold," this yellow flower is actually a member of the daisy family. The flowers can be mashed with oil to produce a salve that slows bleeding and promotes healing in open wounds. In fact, calendula flowers were used in battlefield medicine during both the Civil War and World War I.

Raspberry. You know this fruit is delicious fresh or in preserves. But you might not know that raspberry leaves make a nutritious tea, rich in iron and calcium, that serves as a uterine tonic. It's a traditional remedy for menstrual cramps, and is sometimes given to ease labor pains.

Echinacea. Also known as purple coneflower, this daisylike bloom grows wild throughout the eastern and midwestern United States. Native Americans have long gathered echinacea for its ability to boost the immune system. Taken as a tea or ground up in capsules, it helps to fight colds and flu. Echinacea can also be worked into a salve for external use, to ward off infection from cuts and scrapes.

Goldenseal. The root and leaves of this flower, a relative of the buttercup, are loaded with *hydrastine* and *berberine*—both natural antibiotics. Chop and simmer the root to make a tincture that can be used as a mouth rinse or a topical antiseptic to fight fungal infections such as athlete's foot and ringworm. When taken orally in conjunction with garlic, it's reportedly effective against parasites.

St. John's wort. This five-petaled yellow flower is native to Europe, but has been introduced all over the world, growing wild in some places as an invasive weed. It can be identified by the small oil glands that dot its leaves, giving them a windowed appearance. Crushing the flower buds or seed pods produces a purplish-red liquid with strong anti-inflammatory properties. St. John's wort also boosts the brain's production of melatonin and serotonin and is commonly prescribed for treatment of insomnia and clinical depression.

Ginger. There's a reason your mom gave you ginger ale when you were sick. Ginger root is effective against gastric distress. To soothe nausea, dice ginger finely and boil in water until the infusion takes on a pale golden color. Strain it, and then sweeten the brew with honey if you like (and if you're feeling adventurous, see page 32), and sip either hot or cold. If you don't have the means to prepare a brew, a slice of fresh ginger is just as effective, if a little spicy. The plant is very tough and fibrous when raw, so don't actually swallow it—just chew to extract the juice.

Bark. Being hungry is kind of a medical condition, right? Treat it with the edible inner bark of the eastern white pine. Dry the long, sticky sheets, and then roast to make a crunchy treat, or grind into flour.

HOW TO CATCH A FISH WITH YOUR BARE HANDS

Because only tools need tools.

WHAT YOU'LL NEED

• Because of its inherent dangers, hand fishing should be your last resort in a survival situation. Even if you're stranded with only the clothes on your back, you may be able to come up with improvised fishing tackle from materials at hand.

• The simplest tool is a pointed stick, but spearfishing is difficult to master, demanding both endless patience and lightning reflexes. Although a springy branch can serve as a fishing rod, it's hard to find a workable substitute for fishing line. Ordinary string or sewing thread will likely break the moment you get a strike. Dental floss will work in a pinch; it's surprisingly strong, especially if you braid two strands together. Fashion your hook from a safety pin, or even a thorn.

• For the amateur angler, though, the most effective survival tool is a T-shirt. Roll the sleeves in toward the neck, making a triangle. Tie off the triangle's point tightly. Then poke a few holes in the bottom hem and weave a supple branch through, making a half-hoop that will hold the bottom of the shirt open. In just minutes, you've got a handy fishing net and are ready to catch some supper.

HOW TO DO IT

1. Before you can catch a fish, of course, you and it have to be in the same place. There are two ways to make that happen: either go to where the fish are, or make them come to you. The latter option is a lot less hazardous for the angler, and is reputed to be quite effective for catching brook trout. Look for a spot along the bank where the water is relatively deep and the current is slow. Lie down on your side, with one arm in the water. Get comfortable, because you're going to be there a while.

2. Before you can catch anything, you've got to let your arm go cold. Fish can detect your body heat, and will avoid you until your skin cools to match the ambient temperature.

3. Wiggle your fingers slowly and gently to mimic the movement of a distressed insect.

4. When a fish approaches, stay cool. Move your hand slowly into position under the fish. Some practitioners recommend rubbing your fingers along the fish's belly to hypnotize it—a practice known as "tickling"—but you're in a life-or-death situation, and there's no time for finesse. Just get your palm under the fish, fingers curled upward.

5. Don't try to close your fist—the fish will most likely slip through. Instead, form a scoop with your hand and, in one quick motion, flip the fish up onto the bank.

6. If you're after catfish, the technique of choice is "noodling." This works best in late spring and early summer—spawning season, when catfish stay close to their eggs. You'll have to wade full into the stream or pond and stake out a spot near a nest to await your prey. When  a catfish comes close, don't try to grab the body. You're looking to hook your fingers into the gills, just behind the head; there's enough bone and cartilage there to afford you a solid grip.

* * *

A SHOCKING TALE

On November 9, 1967, 17-year-old Brian Litasa touched a live "ultra-high-voltage" power line in Los Angeles. Estimated shock: 230,000 volts. It's the largest electric shock ever received by a human...who lived through it.

HOW TO GET LOST (AND NOT GO CRAZY)

So you're lost in the wilderness, and you've gotten the whole "food and shelter" thing figured out. Great job! But now you've got way more free time than you can handle. Talking to trees can get pretty tedious. If they start talking back, however, that's a good sign you might *be losing your mind.*

PLAY GOLF IN YOUR HEAD

You've probably heard the widely circulated legend about an American POW who prevented himself from going crazy by playing an imaginary round of golf every day during his incarceration. Once he returned to the United States, he discovered that his real game had greatly improved....or so the story goes. While the identity of the serviceman has never been confirmed, and the entire legend could be bullplop, that doesn't mean that you can't do the same. Visualize a 9- or 18-hole golf course in your mind. Imagine yourself teeing off at each hole and pretend you're playing and employing various strategies. What club should you use on the hole with the water hazard, for example? Each day, add a twist. Maybe it's very breezy, or you're stuck with an irritating caddy like Bill Murray's character from *Caddyshack*. Try out different golf courses or, if you get bored, let your imagination run wild. Picture Godzilla stomping his way across the greens with everybody still playing.

ACTUALLY PLAY GOLF

You don't need fancy clubs or tees to play "wilderness golf." Just grab a stick and a pinecone. Dig some holes and do your best to keep score if you want. If you're really feeling ambitious, you can construct your own miniature golf course. Build ramps out of old branches. Lean them up against tree stumps with holes carved into them. Again, let your imagination run wild. Constructing a windmill hazard, complete with a spinning turbine powered by the wind, should eat up plenty of time while you're waiting for that rescue helicopter to show up.

STICK TO A ROUTINE

Many prisoners who have been subjected to solitary confinement say that maintaining a daily routine kept them from losing it while they were in "the hole." Some began every day of their confinement by washing and tidying up their cell. Others created a complex exercise regimen that involved sit-ups, push-ups, etc. You can do the same to impose structure and order on your chaotic surroundings. Maybe do a few laps around the nearest lake, or use a strong branch to do pull-ups every morning. Prepare your meals at the same time every day. Do the same when it comes to waking up every morning and going to bed each night.

"HOST" A TALK SHOW

Another drawback of too much isolation is that you may find yourself not only losing your sanity, but your cognitive abilities and memory skills as well. To combat this, you can sing, recall the plots of your favorite films, or work out mathematical equations in your head. An all-purpose technique to keep yourself from going crazy while keeping your thinking skills lean and mean? Pretend that you've just landed a sweet gig hosting *The Tonight Show*. You'll need to create skits and come up with questions for each of your imaginary guests. They can range from actors like Channing Tatum and Jennifer Lawrence to eggheads such as Neil deGrasse Tyson and Bill Nye the Science Guy. Your guests don't need to be alive either. Interview Abraham Lincoln or Attila the Hun! Chat with these guests about their latest projects, the weather, how to grow the perfect beard, the meaning of existence....you name it. You'll also need a musical act to conclude each "show." Who better to handle that than yourself? Pretend you're Freddie Mercury and belt out "Bohemian Rhapsody," or see how many of Kanye West's rhymes you can remember. With any luck, you'll draw a "studio audience" of deer and other bemused critters every night.

* * *

DENTAL HEALTH IN THE WILDERNESS

• Chewing on the gum of a pine or spruce tree is a natural way to clean teeth.

• One end of a soft willow twig smoothed down makes an excellent makeshift toothbrush.

• And if those tips don't work: Chewing on clover can help ease the pain of a toothache.

HOW TO BUILD A SHELTER ALMOST ANYWHERE

If you find yourself stranded somewhere, lack of shelter will likely kill you before lack of water does. There are a variety of climates on planet Earth, but if you know what you're doing, you can build yourself a shelter to survive any of them.

IN THE WOODS

1. Locate a tree, rock, or other large object with a clear area beside it. Avoid ditches or other low-lying areas, which may be prone to flooding.

2. Gather branches, sticks, and leaves. If you have an axe, you can cut some down, but you will likely be able to find suitable materials that are down already. You will need a variety of sizes of branches.

3. Lean your largest branch against the rock, tree, etc. You will be building a lean-to type shelter, and this branch will be the frame.

4. Lean smaller branches along either side of the central frame, creating a triangle-shaped, tentlike structure big enough for you to crawl under.

5. Layer leaves and twigs on top of the branches, eventually filling in all of the holes. A top layer of green leaves, or even muddy leaves, will provide a (somewhat) watertight seal.

IN THE TROPICS

Like the woods, a tropical environment provides a variety of resources you can use to construct a shelter. But because the environment may be crawling with snakes and insects, you will need to get your shelter up off the ground.

1. Build a foundation for your shelter. If possible, sink four (or more) short, sturdy branches into the ground, parallel to each other.

2. Lay branches between the posts to create a frame, and then lay other branches across those to create an elevated bed. If you don't have the materials for this, build a "mattress" by piling a nest of twigs and branches until it's 6 to 12 inches thick.

3. Erect the posts that will support your roof. On either side of your shelter, sink sturdy branches that are forked at the top. The parallel branches need to be roughly comparable in height, and the height of each pair of branches should gradually taper so water will run off the roof.

4. Lay long branches between the forked posts, and then line other branches across those— similar to the method for creating the raised bed.

5. Use vines or sturdy grass to lash the branches together.

6. Cover your shelter with leaves, grass, hay, or whatever is available. As in the forest, it's a good idea to top your shelter with a layer of green leaves to make it more waterproof.

7. In the tropics, it's also a good idea to ring your campsite with a layer of banana (or other) leaves. These won't prevent jungle predators from approaching, but at least the rustling in the leaves will alert you to their presence.

IN THE DESERT

Okay, your outlook is getting a little more bleak. A desert environment will be much more barren of natural resources, and the grueling sunlight will incapacitate you much more quickly. But don't despair! There's still a slim chance you can build yourself a shelter before you succumb to madness.

1. Dig yourself a hole. With no trees to provide shade, you'll need to go underground. Dig a trench deep enough that you can lie in it: approximately 18-24 inches. You'll save yourself some work if you can dig alongside a rock or sand dune.

2. You really need some kind of a tarp or blanket. Lay that tarp or blanket over your trench and weigh it down along the rim of the trench with rocks or sand. Then crawl under your shelter and wait for the sun to go down.

3. If you don't have a tarp or blanket, you might be able to carve a small dugout alongside a rock or sand dune, which you could crawl into and partially get yourself

out of the sun. But really, if you haven't brought some material you can use to cover a shelter, you will be less "building a shelter" and more "looking for shade."

THE ARCTIC

The Arctic is perhaps the harshest of all environments—its extreme cold may kill you even faster than the unyielding sun of the desert. That said, snow and ice can provide you with building tools for a shelter...but it takes time. If there are evergreen trees, you can dig out a snow trench at the base of a tree, then line the top and inside of the trench with more evergreen branches. If no trees are available and you need a shelter quickly, your best bet is to build a snow cave.

1. Find a snowdrift at least five feet tall, or if none are available, pile existing snow into a dome.

2. If you have to pile the snow yourself, you'll need to let it sit and harden for at least two hours when you're done, or it will be too loose to dig your cave.

3. Dig a tunnel into the snowdrift or pile. In a real pinch, just crawling into this tunnel can provide rudimentary shelter. But this could also be the beginning of your snow cave.

4. From inside the tunnel, begin hollowing out the inside of the cave. How much space you will have depends on how big the snowbank/pile was to begin with. Leave the roof and sides of the cave at least one foot thick, so as to reduce the likelihood of collapse. You can sink ski poles or whatever else you have on hand into the top of the snow pile to give you a guideline so you don't hollow out too much.

5. Use the Buddy System! If you are with someone, take turns carving out the tunnel and cave. That way, if it collapses on you, there is someone there to save you!

6. Insulate the cave with whatever you can. If any branches are available, lay them over the top and along the floor of the cave. If you have plenty of water, pour some over the top of the cave to further harden it.

7. Once you've created the basic chamber to sustain life, get creative! Snow is a pliable and sturdy building material. You might carve yourself a bench or sleeping area. One good idea is to build yourself a sleeping area elevated from the tunnel entrance, allowing warm air to remain inside.

* * *

HOW TO HIGH-DIVE INTO WATER

• While in the air, keep your body as vertical as possible. Point your toes downward and protect your crotch with your hands. Also clench your buttocks to keep water from rushing in and causing internal damage.

• Once you're in the water, fan out your arms and legs to slow your descent.

HOW TO FIND WILD CAFFEINE

You're the lone survivor of a plane crash over the ocean. You've dragged your battered body ashore to a deserted island with no way to contact the outside world, and you will live out your days completely alone. Sounds like you could use a pick-me-up!

• Somewhere between 60 and 100 plant species are known to produce caffeine. Most temperate regions of the world have *some* native plant that produces the stimulant.

• The caffeine will be in either the plant's seed or nut, as is the case with the coffee plant or kola nut, or in the leaves, as with various varieties of tea. So odds are good that somewhere, wherever you've been deserted, there's a plant that contains caffeine.

• The problem is that many plants that contain caffeine also have other toxic compounds, such as theobromine, which can be poisonous in large doses. While the nut of the kola tree produces caffeine, its leaves produce cocaine, which probably isn't ideal. So this whole caffeine hunt has the potential to go sideways on you. (Caffeine itself exists in plants as a natural pesticide that kills predator insects, so its very genesis is to be toxic.)

• Of course, you're much more likely to stumble on a plant that is *only* toxic, and caffeine-free. If you really need that morning fix, sample small bits of the leaves and beans of various plants, and avoid those that make you hallucinate or violently ill.

• The yaupon holly, which grows in the Southwestern U.S., was long used by the Choctaw, Cherokee, and other indigenous peoples to induce vomiting. (The plant's scientific name: *Ilex vomitoria*.) However, the caffeine-rich plant doesn't induce vomiting if made into a mild tea. Simply steam and roast the leaves, then steep.

• Once you've found a plant that produces caffeine, extracting it is relatively simple. You can simply chew on the leaves or nut, as is done in many African cultures, or steep them in hot water. If the taste is unpleasant, consider also steeping some native fruit or berries along with it. (Just be sure the berries aren't toxic either.)

HOW TO GET ASPIRIN FROM A TREE

Because getting lost in the woods is a real headache!

HOW TO DO IT

1. Find a willow tree. There are over 400 varieties of willows (and their narrow-leafed shrub cousins, the osiers) that grow throughout the Northern Hemisphere, and they all contain a compound called salicin in their bark sap. The human body metabolizes salicin into salicylic acid—the active ingredient in aspirin. To prepare a headache remedy, prepare a tea from willow bark. Any kind of willow will do, but the white willow is favored (it was a favorite of the Cherokee) because its bark contains an unusually high concentration of salicin.

2. With a knife, cut a square of bark about the size of your hand. Don't worry about hurting the tree; it can grow back a patch this size in less than six months.

3. Pry the bark off carefully. There will be an inner layer with a faint pink tinge. Cut or scrape this layer away from the bark. Some of it may cling to the tree; scrape that away, too.

4. Gather up your palmful of bark scraps and pop them into about a pint of boiling water. Let the mixture boil for about 20 minutes, then let cool and steep for a few minutes after.

5. The resulting infusion will be a dark brown-red. Pour it off, filtering out the solids through a cloth, and drink it down.

So how well does this homemade aspirin work? For minor aches and pains, it's fairly effective, though not as strong as the version from the drugstore. And the potential for side effects—including irritation or bleeding of the stomach, nausea, and bloody stools—is more pronounced than for the synthetic stuff. Still, you'd probably have to drink several cups of willow brew before you started seeing any ill effects.

BARKING MAD

• Stomach upset from your homebrewed aspirin? Never fear—chewing the inner bark of the yellow birch (*Betula allegheniensis*) is a Micmac remedy for indigestion and stomach cramps. Indeed, many tree barks have medicinal or practical applications.

• Birch bark had a multitude of uses for Native Americans. It was thin enough to use as paper, but tough enough to skin a canoe. Because of its waterproof qualities, it was often used to make buckets or cups.

• The bark of the cinchona tree, native to Peru, is a major source of quinine, the antibacterial substance that's useful both for fighting malaria and in making a delicious gin and tonic. Quinine is also found in the common American dogwood (*Cornus florida*).

• The Ojibway people use a tea made from the bark of the tamarack (*Larix laricina*) as a gargle to treat sore throats.

• Bark from the alder (*Alnus oblongifolia*) will produce a tincture reputed to boost the immune system and fight inflammation.

• The African cherry tree (*Pygeum africanum*) contains in its bark phytosterols that can help to treat prostate trouble.

• The xylem in tree bark allows sap to flow through but blocks tiny particles and bubbles. These qualities make bark a natural alternative for water filtration. In laboratory tests, filters made of white pine sapwood caught 99% of bacteria.

HOW TO EAT HUMAN FLESH

Okay, so eating people probably isn't your plan A. But dire circumstances can arise when your only other option is to starve. So if things ever go really sideways on you, here's what you need to know.

BUTCHERING

Commercially produced pigs and cows have been bred to produce maximum meat. A comparable cut from the pilot who couldn't guide that Cessna through bad weather will not be as meaty. A tip: Go for the legs. Rotate the leg around in the hip joint as you saw through, and eventually you should hear a "pop" and be able to pull the leg free. You may also want to separate the lower leg at the knee bone for easier preparation. Avoid eating the liver and kidneys because they filter waste and could be toxic.

PREPARATION

Be creative! Most any beef or pork recipe could be modified to work with people. But remember, this is not the commercially produced fare you are used to, which is raised for its tenderness and butchered young. The average Dale will be tougher and more stringy than what you're used to. For that reason, consider a braise. The long, slow cook time and the added liquid should maximize the flavor and texture.

FLAVOR

The meat on your average Gary looks most similar to beef, but most people who have actually eaten people (Polynesian cannibals, interviewed by ethnologists, for example) say it tastes more like pork. So adjust your recipe accordingly.

EMOTIONAL TRAUMA

By this point, you've seen and done some things that can't be unseen or undone. It's likely that those images, sounds, and smells will haunt you. When you get back to civilization, you will want to seek out professional psychiatric help.

HOW TO LOOK YOUR BEST OUT THERE

Ignoring primping and pampering because you're too busy struggling to find food and shelter? Here's how to look your best when that hunky rescue crew arrives.

SKIN CARE

Needless to say, you're not going to find any bottles of Clinique Intense Skin Fortifying Hydrator out there. To help keep your skin looking and feeling fantastic, the best thing you can do is stay out of the sun as much as possible—a bad burn is *not* going to do you any favors. If you're heading into a desert region, you're going to need to make some "wilderness suntan lotion" to cover up any exposed skin. If you have access to water, mix it with soil and make some muddy sunblock. The alkaline dust that covers many playas and deserts in the U.S. will help protect your skin from the sun, but it will also suck moisture out of it like a sponge. If you can, bring along (or locate) some aloe vera plants and use the gel-like substance in their leaves to soothe any dry spots. Witch hazel, jellyweed, and chickweed will also work as natural substitutes for your favorite moisturizer back home.

A BEAUTIFUL SMILE

Even if you're planning to be rescued within a week or two, don't forget to brush your teeth. Only a few days of plaque buildup can leave your teeth looking like a jack o' lantern's. If you left your electric toothbrush and dental floss at home, don't worry. Makeshift toothpicks, made out of bits of birch, can work wonders. Table salt and baking soda, if you have them, can be used as toothpaste in a pinch, but don't be afraid to scrape your teeth with your fingernails if all else fails. (Clean them first, of course, and after.) Wilderness survival types also say that you can use charcoal from a campfire to clean your teeth. While it might taste even worse than that weird organic toothpaste from the health food store, grind the charcoal into dust, wipe it against your teeth, and let its corrosiveness wipe away all that pesky gunk. Another tip: Rinse your mouth with water after every meal.

WILDERNESS MAKEUP

• **Eye shadow.** While you may have heard that eyeliner is made out of bat guano, don't go stomping off into any caves in search of some. Why? Because it's a widespread myth...that could give you a nasty bacterial infection. Instead, try soot, which can also work as a substitute for eye shadow. Ancient Egyptians used *kohl*, a substance made out of lead and some other ingredients, but all that could be hard to come by in the great outdoors.

• **Lipstick.** Queen Elizabeth I popularized lipstick in England, and in the 16th century, it was made out of beeswax and crushed wild berries. You should be able to whip some up without too much trouble, aside from a dozen or so bee stings.

• **Blush.** Try drying any leftover berries, crushing them, and mixing them with a bit of dry dirt for rouge. In a pinch, you could always pinch your cheeks to help them look their rosiest, too. It's a trick that has worked for "ladies of the night" for centuries.

YOUR HAIR, OUT THERE

As any dog will tell you, hair can and will attract fleas, not to mention bacteria and parasites. If it seems like your rescuers may be awhile, trim your hair down to at least shoulder length. Keeping your hair combed and as clean as possible will help you look and feel fabulous. If you don't have any Herbal Essences laying around, whip up some "wilderness shampoo." If you're in an arid or desert area, dig up a small to medium-sized yucca plant, shake off the dirt, and chop the roots into small pieces, then pound them into a pulp. When the color turns from white to light amber, you're good to go.

PLANTS YOU MUST NOT TOUCH

So you've learned to reliably identify poison ivy, poison oak, poison sumac, and all their urushiol-bearing, itch-producing relatives in the Toxicodendron genus, eh? Congratulations! Here's a rundown of a few other poisonous plants to give you nightmares.

OLEANDER

This ornamental evergreen can be found across the southern U.S., and is often planted along highway medians in California and Texas. Oleander can grow into small trees nearly 20 feet tall. The narrow, blade-shaped leaves are tough and leathery, surrounding clusters of five-petaled pink-and-white flowers. The sap can cause irritation to the skin and eyes, while ingesting the leaves can bring on nausea and bloody diarrhea.

NETTLES

This family of plants—perennials that can grow to six feet high, with broad sawtoothed leaves on a wiry green stem—has long been used as animal feed and in traditional medicine. But don't try picking it without gloves. The leaves and stems have needle-like stinging hairs that carry histamine, causing allergic inflammation and itching. Interestingly, grasping a nettle firmly can crush the hairs flat, and may actually do less damage than brushing lightly against the plant.

GIANT HOGWEED

Introduced to the Western Hemisphere from central Asia as an ornamental plant, this invasive noxious weed is like something out of a horror movie. Standing up to 18 feet tall, giant hogweed is surrounded by clusters of broad bright-green leaves that may grow up to five feet wide, rising to an umbrella-shaped head of tiny white flowers; the appearance has been described as "Queen Anne's lace on steroids." The sap of the plant is phototoxic—meaning that its poison is activated by light. Initial contact may cause simple redness and itching. The severity of the symptoms increases with continued exposure to sunlight or UV rays; the damage peaks within 48 hours with the appearance of huge, painful blisters that form into black or purplish scars. Giant hogweed toxin actually bonds with the DNA of the skin tissue cells, killing them from the inside and producing excess melanin—the resulting scars and discoloration can take years to fade. Even more frightening: Trace amounts of giant hogweed sap in the eyes can cause permanent blindness. The plant is widespread across Europe and the British Isles, but has thus far only been found in pockets across North America, where there are concentrated efforts to eradicate it.

ACONITE

This grows in mountain meadows and can be distinguished by its tall-stemmed, helmet-shaped flowers. Even casual contact can be deadly because the alkaloid neurotoxin is easily absorbed through the skin. The effects begin with a tingling and numbness at the contact site, spreading gradually up the arm to the shoulder. Death from asphyxiation occurs within hours, as the poison paralyzes the heart and lungs.

HOW TO AVOID LIGHTNING

Lightning kills around 2,000 people every year, leaves many more with debilitating injuries, and almost never bestows people with awesome superpowers. So you should best avoid it.

ELECTRIC BOOGALOO

• The uniqueness of weather patterns makes lightning very rare over the North and South Poles, as well as far out at sea. So if you really want to go out of your way to avoid lightning, you could live in those places. Otherwise, one of the safest places to be during an electrical storm is inside a car. The metal exterior of a car acts like a Faraday cage, conducting the electricity around the outside of the vehicle, and into the ground instead of into you. On the downside, if the lightning storm progresses into a tornado, the car turns into one of the least safe places to be.

• A modern house or building that is electrically grounded is a pretty safe place to be, with a few caveats. Avoid taking a shower or bath, as it's

possible for the electrical charge to move through the metal plumbing, and then through the water itself. If you happen to live in the year 1999 and still use a landline telephone, you'll want to avoid that too, because the charge can move through the phone line.

• So what if you're outside when bolts of electricity come shooting out of the sky? Well, you are certainly in a more dangerous situation, but there are still measures you can take to stay safe.

IF OUTSIDE IN A STORM:

• Do not stand under tall trees, power lines, and other large objects. The tree branches may keep you dry from the rain, but tall objects are more likely to draw lightning.

• If you are out in the open, crouch low to the ground, on the balls of your feet, and put your heels together. Do not lie down—the charge from a lightning strike may move along the surface of the ground. By putting your heels together, it's possible that a charge that enters through one foot will exit through the other and go back into the ground, rather than passing through your body and frying your guts.

• Take notice if your hair begins to stand on end or you feel your skin tingling. These are signs that a lightning strike is imminent. It's kind of like having spider sense, which is pretty awesome, except it means you are about to be struck by lightning. If you aren't already crouching, get down fast!

• The electrical shock often causes cardiac arrest, so you may need to do CPR. Some people who remain conscious may not even realize they have been struck, but because the electrical charge affects the central nervous system, be on the lookout for anyone who complains of dizziness, headache, or nausea or who seems generally confused. Have the person lie down and remain still until help arrives.

HOW TO MAKE A LOINCLOTH

After a year or five in the wilderness, your clothing is probably going to start looking a little raggedy. When you're on the verge of exposing your private parts to the Great Outdoors, it's time to make a loincloth.

WHAT YOU'LL NEED

- A beaver or nutria
- Skinning tools
- Knife
- Thin branch
- Twine
- Fire

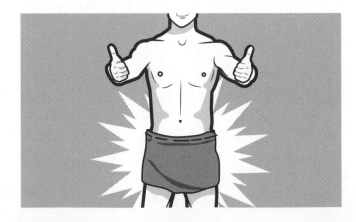

160

HOW TO DO IT

1. First, you'll need to kill a critter that has enough fur and skin to cover your naughty bits. We're not saying you're fat, but a squirrel probably won't get the job done; you're better off with a larger fuzzy mammal, like a beaver or a nutria.

2. After you've killed the critter, skin it and feel free to use the rest of its body for food or toolmaking (see page 235). Next, you'll need to clean the pelt. There are a few different ways you can do this. If you're near a lake or stream that's populated with fish, place it in the water and allow the fish to nibble away all the remaining tissue and fat. Leave it overnight, but be sure to secure it to the shoreline first. If you're in a hurry, you can clean the pelt with a knife or the sharp edge of something.

3. Now you'll need a wooden loop that will help you dry the pelt. Make one out of a thin and bendable tree branch. Stretch the pelt and tie it within the loop with twine (this can be thin strips of dried animal skin or makeshift twine

harvested from a fibrous plant). It should be taut, like a drumhead.

4. Place the pelt near a fire and wait until the skin is dry. Clean off any still-lingering tissue or other icky stuff. The pelt's skin should be smooth to the touch. When it feels like the sort of thing you wouldn't mind touching your most sensitive areas, it's time to turn the pelt into a loincloth.

5. Wrap the pelt around your pelvic area and adjust it until it feels comfortable. If the pelt fits well, connect the ends together with some twine and tie them.

6. Bounce around a bit and/or take a quick jog. You'll want to make sure that your new loincloth won't fall off at an awkward moment (like while you're trying to defend yourself from a bloodthirsty cougar, for example).

7. It's the perfect thing to wear when playing Tarzan (see page 71).

HOW TO MAKE WATERPROOF MATCHES

Anyone can make a fire with two sticks—so long as one of your sticks is a wooden match. If your matches get wet, though, forget it. Luckily, waterproofing your matches is fairly easy. The principle is simple: Coat the match head and part of the stick with a substance that will repel water, but won't smother the flame once the match is struck. You have a choice of materials, each of which calls for a slightly different technique.

WHAT YOU'LL NEED

- Beeswax or paraffin
- Double boiler
- Twine
- Kitchen tongs
- Baking rack
- Newspaper
- Clear nail polish
- Turpentine
- Glass jar

THE WAX METHOD

Although you could use candle drippings, a safer method is to melt your wax—either beeswax or paraffin—in a double boiler, preferably one you never plan to use again for food. Tie the matches in a bundle with twine. Use your tongs to dip the bundle into the melted wax to about a third of the matches' length. Separate the bundle, and cool the matches on a rack with newspaper underneath to catch the drips. Store in a waterproof container.

THE NAIL POLISH METHOD

Brush a light coat of clear polish onto each match, covering about a third of its length—the sulfur head and a couple of centimeters below. Dry on a rack. Store in a waterproof container.

THE TURPENTINE METHOD

While wax and nail polish are the two most common waterproofing agents for matches, turpentine is the cooler alternative. Because turpentine actually drives off moisture, it can even be used to revive matches spoiled by damp. Pour out a few tablespoons of turpentine into a glass jar or ceramic dish—it can eat through plastic. Insert the matches headfirst; soak for five minutes. Let dry on newspaper for 30 minutes. Unlike matches waterproofed by other methods, which can be stored indefinitely, turpentined matches will need to be retreated every few months.

A FEW MORE TIPS

• Even if you don't go to the trouble of waterproofing your matches, if you're serious at all about wilderness survival, you'll at least want to make sure your matches are packed in a waterproof container. Camping goods stores sell screwtop plastic jobbies for this purpose, but unless you're on a rafting trip or are otherwise likely to get completely soaked, a plastic 35-mm film canister will suffice.

• Don't forget to keep a striking surface in there, too. A scrap of fine-grit sandpaper or an emery board will do nicely, and may prove more portable than the original matchbox.

HOW TO MAKE A GUN

Perhaps you're stuck in an abandoned shack in the middle of the woods and there's a bear coming at you. You gotta do what you gotta do.

WHAT YOU'LL NEED

- Metal pipe or tube
- Block of wood
- A nail
- .22-caliber ammunition
- Rubber bands or a Spring

HOW TO DO IT

1. Find an appropriate barrel. This will be the most important piece of your gun. You will want some kind of metal pipe or tube that you can fit a .22-caliber bullet inside. A pipe from underneath a sink, the leg from a metal folding chair—anything like that will do.

2. Attach your barrel to a block of wood (using glue is fine), leaving you a flat wooden surface

at least a couple inches long behind the back of your barrel. You will use this wood surface to build your firing mechanism.

3. File down the tip of a nail, so it no longer comes to such a sharp point. This will serve as your firing pin.

4. Attach your rubber bands or spring to the wood block. You will be using these to pull back your nail and propel it into the bullet at the opening of your barrel. Rubber bands will be easiest, though they may not always strike in exactly the same location. Mounting a spring will be more consistent, but may require a bit of extra hardware.

5. Place your .22-caliber round into the back of the barrel. (You can use any size of ammunition, but a .22 is recommended because of the smaller size of both the round and the explosion.)

6. Fire! Pull back your rubber band or spring and release. The striker/firing pin will make contact with the cap, which in turn will propel the bullet out of the barrel.

7. If all goes well, you've just fired your own homemade gun, and there's at least a reasonable chance you haven't blown your hand off in the process.

* * *

HOW TO MAKE WATER IN THE FOREST

Even if the climate is hospitable, like in a forest, you can only survive for around three days without water. Luckily for you, water all around us. You can extract water from green leaves.

Let's assume you forgot to bring water with you to the wilderness, but you did bring a plastic bag. Put the bag around the green leaves at the end of a tree branch. Seal the bag tightly, tying it off with a paracord or something similar. The green leaves will release water through condensation, and the plastic bag will prevent that water vapor from being released into the air. As the day goes on, those drips of condensation will begin to pool inside the bag. By sundown, you may have as much as a cup of water.

HOW TO MAKE BULLETS

Killing a delicious or ferocious beast with a gun you made yourself (see page 166) will fill you with a sense of pride and industriousness. But to really earn the title "Do-It-Yourselfer," shouldn't you also make your own bullets? Of course you should. In fact, before the Industrial Age, this is what they did in the Old West.

WHAT YOU'LL NEED

- Electric or gas stove
- 5-6 pounds of lead
- A large, durable cauldron
- Ventilation mask
- Candle wax
- Crayons
- A metal ladle
- Bullet mold
- Lubricant

HOW TO DO IT

1. First, you'll need to get your hands on some actual lead. That's not as easy these days, because the government has restricted the use of lead in most applications because it's really poisonous if handled incorrectly. (That stuff in pencils? It's graphite, not lead.) Still, you can probably find some at a local scrap metal yard or an auto shop, because lead is commonly used in wheel weights, or in old plumbing parts.

2. It doesn't matter what form the lead is in, because you'll just be melting it down. Turn your stove on full blast, dump your lead into the cauldron, and heat it up. You may want to work outside and try to avoid inhaling the fumes because, again, lead is very poisonous. After about 20 to 30 minutes, you should have molten lead, probably with a little crud floating on the top.

3. You'll need to remove the impurities from the lead through a process called *fluxing*. Simply drop a bit of candle wax (or even

children's crayons) into the molten lead. Stir occasionally with your metal ladle. Any impurities in the mixture will adhere to the wax and eventually rise to the top. Skim that off with your ladle.

4. At this stage, you could pour your molten lead into something like a muffin tin and allow it to cool, forming "ingots." These small, evenly sized bits of alloy can be easily stored and broken down for use later on.

5. Or, you can ladle the molten lead into your bullet mold. Bullet molds have been around for hundreds of years and come in many varieties, but generally they look something like a pair of pliers. Once the lead has been poured inside, pulling the handles seals the mold.

6. After allowing the lead to cool for just a few seconds, open the mold. Most bullet molds will also shave off any excess from the still-soft lead as they open.

7. You can drop the bullets either onto a towel or into a bucket of water to cool. We suggest

the water, because it will make a cool sizzling sound.

8. Homemade, unjacketed bullets need to be lubricated or they will leave lead residue in the barrel of your gun, and who wants that? Simply squirt a little of your lubricant of choice onto each bullet and allow it to dry.

9. Just like that, you've taken a highly poisonous metal and turned it into a lethal projectile!

* * *

HOW TO ESCAPE BEING TIED UP

Although this rarely occurs outside the movies, it does happen. If it happens to you, here's a neat magician's trick (Houdini used it) that may help you escape: While your captor is tying you up, make yourself as large as possible by inhaling and pushing your chest out. Flex any muscles that are being tied up, but do it as subtly as possible so as not to raise suspicion. When your captor leaves, relax. You'll get at least a half an inch of slack in the ropes, which should be more than enough for you to wiggle your way to freedom.

LOSE A LIMB, SAVE YOUR LIFE

So you're out rock climbing or hiking on the side of a cliff, and lose your foothold, and oops—you've got an arm or a leg lodged between two heavy, gigantic, immovable rocks. If it's too remote to call for help, or you're worried animals may attack you, or that you'll eventually die from starvation or exposure, you've got to do what you've got to do: Leave that limb behind for the sake of survival.

WHAT YOU'LL NEED

- A heavy rock that you can manage with one hand
- A pocketknife
- Pliers (if you've got them)
- A belt or scarf to use as a tourniquet
- Wrapping cloth
- Actual courage
- Liquid courage, such as a slug of whiskey (if you've got some in your flask)

HOW TO DO IT

1. If you've gotten yourself stuck in rocky terrain, chances are there are small, lose rocks within arm's reach. Find a rock that's manageable in one hand (if you need to free a stuck arm) or with two (if you need to free a leg).

2. Take the rock and smash the bones in your trapped limb, breaking them fully apart, or to the best of your ability. This will make the limb looser and easier to work with.

3. Determine where you will need to cut the limb off—no more than necessary. Tie a tourniquet three inches or so above the cut site—your belt or a scarf or another piece of

174

cloth should work well. Tie it tight—this will prevent you from bleeding to death when you sever any arteries.

4. With your pocketknife, saw through your skin and muscles. Try to avoid cutting through major arteries for as long as possible, to prevent blood loss.

5. The tendons will be especially tough to cut through with the pocketknife. If you have pliers, use them to snap the tendons apart.

6. Cut through those arteries now.

7. While all that was unfathomably painful, it's not nearly as horrible as what comes next: snip through the nerves in the limb with the pocketknife.

8. Cut through any remaining bits of gristle or any bones that are still attached.

9. Remove the tourniquet, and wrap your stump in whatever nonbloodied cloth you've got.

10. Now that you're free, seek medical attention immediately.

HOW TO ACQUIRE STOCKHOLM SYNDROME

Survival isn't always about boiling tree bark and eating bugs. Sometimes it's a deeply frightening psychological game—play your cards right, and you'll stay safe.

STUCK TOGETHER

• A hostage situation is emotionally intense for everyone, captors and captives alike. Theoretically, the captor dominates the power dynamic, but in practice, with everyone stuck in a confined space, in a pressure-cooker atmosphere—after a while, people start to connect.

• These connections—which psychologists call "capture bonding"—take many forms. In the 1973 incident that gave Stockholm syndrome its name, bank employees held hostage after a botched robbery told negotiators that they felt safe with their captors, and they pleaded with police, and a later a judge, to let the gunmen go free. (They weren't set free.) Newspaper heiress Patty Hearst, kidnapped in 1974 by the self-styled revolutionaries of the Symbionese Liberation Army, came to espouse their ideology and even helped them commit further crimes. The bonds of connection can work in both directions: When the Japanese ambassadorial residence in Peru was seized by rebel guerrillas in 1996, the rebels appeared to develop a sort of reverse Stockholm syndrome, releasing most of the hostages on humanitarian grounds.

• Make no mistake: Stockholm syndrome is a toxic psychological condition, and acquiring it may not do much for your long-term mental health. But you're reading this book because you want to survive—and bonding with your captors in a hostage situation might help increase your odds.

HOW TO DO IT

1. **Listen.** Before you can make an emotional connection, you need to signal your emotional availability (or at least fake it). Encourage your captor to open up to you. Don't pry or demand; use neutral phrasing.

As your captor explains the ideology or circumstances that led to you becoming a hostage, resist the temptation to either argue or persuade. *Don't judge. Just listen.* And use phrases like these:

- "I just want to understand why you're doing this."
- "People's Army of Vindication, eh? I'm intrigued."

2. **Empathize.** Whether your captor is a desperate criminal or a crackpot ideologue, chances are he's feeling a bit misunderstood. He's under stress, in danger, and in way over his head. Show him some understanding. You don't have to approve of his ideology or his actions. Just demonstrate sympathy on a basic human level. Useful phrases:

- "It must be frustrating, waiting for the hostage negotiators to call. Don't worry, I'm sure they'll get in touch soon."
- "That People's Army of Vindication flag looks heavy. Don't your arms get tired?"

3. **Reflect.** This is where you'll come up against some tricky ethical lines. Your aim now is to

see your captor as he sees himself—and that means endorsing his beliefs about himself and his cause. Begin with the understanding that no one is a villain to himself. Considering what you've learned of your captor's ideology or criminal past, find ways to reframe it that cast him as either the hero or the victim. Reflect that image back to him. You don't have to flatter him, necessarily—just concede that he has a point.

Warning: This stage may result in your being recruited to the cause or offered a job as getaway driver; follow the dictates of your conscience. Useful phrases:

• "I can't believe they sent you to jail for that. The judge must have had it in for you."

• "Someday, when the People's Army of Vindication has liberated the bourgeoisie, we'll be able to look back on this and laugh."

4. Following this plan, you'll learn to view your captor not as a vicious thug or obsessed fanatic, but as a human being in a bad situation. And with luck, he'll learn to view you the same way.

ANIMALS YOU CANNOT EAT

If you're stranded, be it on a desert island or in the Arctic Circle, your first goal should be to hunt down something to eat. Hooray, you caught something! Before you cook and devour that tasty flesh, you'll want to make sure it's not among the fauna that will kill you if you eat it.

TROPICAL FISH

The warm waters of the tropics are home to a number of fish that will end you should you try to eat them. Many of them have parrotlike beaks with skin that can inflate around their spines, like the well-known blowfish. The puffer's blood and liver are so poisonous that eating even an ounce can be fatal. Several types of jellyfish and octopus are also deadly to eat. The preponderance of poisonous fish in the tropics also has ramifications up the food chain. Predatory fish like barracuda and snapper, while not deadly themselves, can become so after feasting all day on other, poisonous fish.

PLATYPUS

They're warm-blooded and furry, yet they lay eggs like a reptile. They are also poisonous. The platypus has a pair of poisonous spurs on its hind legs, used for defense. While the poison is not generally strong enough to kill an adult human, it can make you seriously ill.

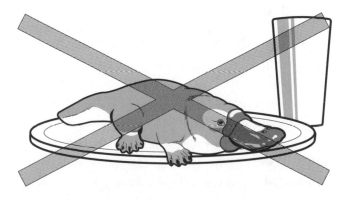

BARRACUDA

In addition to being very vicious and hard to capture, they grow up to five feet in length. While that is a lot of potential meat, there's a reason you can't get a barracuda burger at Five Guys: the fish contains a dangerous toxin called *ciguatera*. Consuming it can cause hallucinations, vertigo, and muscle aches that can last anywhere from a few weeks to several years.

WILD TURTLES

While some turtles are okay to eat—turtle soup is a dated delicacy, for example—others aren't, such as the ones that live in marshy areas that eat poisonous mushrooms. Well, they're not toxic to the turtles, of course, but the poison can stick around in a turtle's body. The older the turtle, the more likely it is to have tons of toxic fungus residue in its flesh that can't even be cooked out. Elsewhere, the hawksbill turtle, which is commonly found in the Atlantic Ocean, has a thorax gland that's downright deadly for humans. On the whole, reptiles can be great a source of protein, but avoid any that have a shell on their backs—like turtles.

HOW TO JUMP OUT OF STUFF

Maybe you fell, maybe you were pushed, or maybe you simply decided to make a hasty exit. In any case, you're in midair, gravity is doing its thing, and you've got an imminent appointment with the ground. How are you going to survive this?

OUT OF AN AIRPLANE

The upside to jumping from an airplane is that you've got plenty of time to plan your landing; 12,000 feet in free fall takes about three minutes.

1. If possible, grab any debris on your way out, like seat cushions or bits of fuselage, to create drag.

2. First, slow your descent by spread-eagling to increase your surface area.

3. If the terrain below is varied, aim for a landing surface that will compress, thereby absorbing your impact. Snow, swampy ground, and haystacks are ideal. (Also helpful: a parachute.)

OFF OF A LEDGE

Leaping from a tall building—we presume it's on fire, and you're not financially devastated by the Stock Market Crash of '29—affords less time to increase your drag.

1. Your best bet is to disperse your impact and break your fall by bumping something on the way down, like a ledge, a flagpole, or a railing. You'll get banged up, but it could save your life.

2. Crashing through something, like an awning or skylight, will also slow you down.

3. Again, aim to land in something that will compress: a pile of boxes, or a Dumpster full of garbage, for example.

4. Try to land on your feet, knees slightly bent, with your hands up to protect your head.

5. Then, throw yourself sideways on impact to distribute the shock of landing sequentially from your feet to your calf, thigh, hip, and back. Skydivers call this a five-point landing. (They also have parachutes. Use one of those if at all possible.)

INTO WATER

Jumping into water from a great height is risky even for a strong swimmer. Water displaces without compressing, so it does little to cushion your impact. A belly flop off a three-foot diving board hurts like hell; from 100 feet, you might as well be diving onto cement.

1. If your getaway plan involves jumping off a cliff into the ocean, try to present as little surface area as possible, entering the water feet first like a knife.

2.   Assume a standing position, knees locked, and toes pointed.

3.   Tuck your chin and lock your fingers on top of your head, elbows held in close to the body.

4.   One good deep breath should give you enough oxygen for a full minute underwater—plenty of time to surface. You may sink as deep as 20 feet; keep your head oriented upward and push up with your arms until your head breaks water.

* * *

HOW TO ESCAPE AN UNRULY MOB

• Stay on your feet and move with the crowd. Stopping for even a second may cause you to lose your footing and get trampled.

• If you are stopped, take a deep breath and tense up your shoulders, biceps, and chest. Bunch your arms up against your stomach to make yourself as solid as possible.

• Keep quiet. You'll call less attention to yourself, which could save you from pepper spray, bullets, and flying fists.

HOW TO REPOPULATE THE EARTH

Good news: You survived the nuclear war. Bad news: Earth's population has been decimated, and all that remains is you and a 22-year-old supermodel. It's up to you to save the human race!

THE BIRDS & BEES

In due time, after a catastrophic event, the Earth could reasonably be repopulated, so long as you carefully promote genetic diversity.

Experts estimate that every person carries the genes for around 5-10 genetic diseases. Luckily, these are recessive traits, so they only manifest when we mate with a partner who carries the same trait. In a diverse population, these diseases are rare. But when everybody is marrying his or her cousin—as in closed communities like Appalachian hill people, European royalty, or your personal postapocalyptic wasteland, they become more common. For example, hemophilia was pervasive among the ruling classes of Europe.

MAKIN' WHOOPEE

You and—depending on your gender—Miss America or Captain America are hopefully genetically distinct going in, so the outlook for your kids is pretty good. But that next generation, beyond the weirdness of having to mate with a sibling, will be at a very high risk for whatever genetic disease traits are present. The old story about inbreeding leading to messed-up kids? It's true. One study found a 20-36% rate of mortality or major disability among children of siblings. If a serious disease manifests itself, it's quite possible that the population could be wiped out in the "genetic bottleneck" of those first two to three generations.

After those first few generations, the risk decreases significantly as long as people procreate with partners separated as far from them as possible. First cousins share only 13% of the same genetic material, and the ratio continues to decrease the further out you go. Bottom line: You're going to want to implement a system of arranged marriage, or at least arranged procreation.

FAMILY TREE

Whether you're starting with a base population of 2 or 10 or 100, you'll want to map it out (perhaps on a cave wall) and pair up newlyweds with partners as far removed, genetically, as possible.

With some careful arrangement of mates and a little luck getting through that initial bottleneck, you'll have the world overfilled, drained of natural resources, and ruled by nations with nuclear stockpiles again in no time!

* * *

SOCKS FOR FOX

One wild animal you don't need to much worry about: the fox. Rarely, if ever, do they attack humans. If threatened, they simply run off. However, if you're sleeping under the stars, be warned that curious foxes are known to gently nibble on exposed human toes.

TRUE TALES OF WEIRD SURVIVAL: JUANA MARIA

ISLAND GIRL

Juana Maria was born in 1811 into the Nicoleño, a small tribe on San Nicolas Island off the coast of California. Tragically, a group of otter hunters massacred most of the group in 1835, leaving behind only a handful of survivors, who were rescued by missionaries from Santa Barbara.

Maria was not among them. A strong storm was moving in, and the missionaries decided to quickly return to the mainland, leaving only her behind. At the time, their resources were thin, and ships along the California coastline were hard to come by. Accidents and complications delayed and eventually canceled further rescue attempts.

Nevertheless, Maria managed to avoid the hunters and continued living on the island in the days that followed. Days turned into months turned into years. Remarkably, she survived another 18 years before she was discovered by a fur trapper named George Nidever.

GEORGE OF THE JUNGLE

After hearing that Maria might still be living on the island, he launched his first attempt to rescue her in 1850; that effort and another both failed. On his third try in 1853, a member of Nidever's search party discovered footprints on a beach and seal blubber that had been left out in the sun to dry. They found Maria living in a small hut constructed of whale bones. She was wearing a dress made of bird feathers that she had sewn together with otter muscle tissue.

By then, all the other Nicoleños had died on the mainland from various causes, leaving her the last living member of her tribe. Nidever transported her back to Santa Barbara, where she died a mere seven weeks after her arrival because of her body's inability to fight off foreign diseases and adjust to a new diet. Before her death, she was baptized and given the name "Juana Maria" by a priest. Her Native American name was, unfortunately, never recorded.

HOW TO GET DRUNK IN THE WOODS

Not only can getting hopelessly stuck in the woods be incredibly dangerous, but it can be incredibly boring too. When your political debates with squirrels start going in circles and running away from hungry bears only makes you yawn, it's time to find a way to get rip-roaring drunk. But how, you ask? Here's a recipe for what we'll call "forest wine."

WHAT YOU'LL NEED

- 5 to 6 pounds of blackberries, or other edible wild berries
- 7 pints of water
- A bowl
- A sealable container, such as a bucket with a lid

- A tube or hose
- A knife
- Something to filter the wine once it's ready, such as a pair of socks

HOW TO DO IT

1. Gather and wash the berries. Wait for them to air dry, and place them in the bowl for three or four days.

2. While you're waiting, clean your sealable container. This will prevent bacteria from growing, which could mess up your wine while it ferments.

3. Remove any moss that has accumulated on your berries and mash them. Dump the berries and their juice into the container and add the water.

4. Cut a hole just large enough for the tube in the top of the container. Close the container and insert the tube. This will allow the carbon dioxide that will develop inside to escape (and prevent your wine from exploding).

5. Place the container in a warm spot (but out of direct sunlight—that's too hot). Now wait a while. This process could take anywhere from a week to a month depending on various conditions.

6. When the time is right, remove the berries and filter the wine. If you're using your socks, be sure to clean them first. There's nothing worse than kicking back with a glass of forest wine only to discover a toenail floating in it.

7. Now it's time to try the wine. You shouldn't expect a "bouquet" or a "balance" worthy of a pinot noir from one of France's finest wineries. Your forest wine is probably going to be pretty disgusting and taste like, well, a bunch of rotten berries that have been sitting in a bucket for several weeks and then filtered through an old sock. Nevertheless, the wine should get you at least a little bit tipsy, maybe even totally wasted.

8. Sip it slowly. If this recipe worked like a charm, the wine could contain high levels of alcohol. Birds and other small animals have been known to succumb to alcohol poisoning from consuming too many fermented berries....which are basically the same thing you're putting in your stomach. (And watch out for any birds and other small animals that might try to steal your wine.)

HOW TO LAND A PLANE IN AN EMERGENCY

Uh-oh. The pilot of your airplane passed out. The copilot parachuted to safety. It's up to you to save the day and guide this death trap to safety! Here's how to do it, by land or by sea.

ON FLAT GROUND

1. Level the plane. Use the outside surroundings to guide you or, if you cannot see clearly, the plane's attitude indicator—it reports the aircraft's relation to the ground. It does not measure your own personal attitude, which is probably on the negative side given that you're in a broken-down aircraft 20,000 feet above the ground.

2. Turn on the radio and let Ground Control know they should get some emergency personnel on the runway, because your

landing won't be perfect. This will (hopefully) be the only time you have to yell "Mayday!" in your life, so have fun with it. Use a British accent.

3. Once you get ground control on the line, they'll help guide you toward the nearest runway. Pull back on the throttle to reduce engine power and activate the aircraft's flaps to help lower your speed.

4. Dump the fuel. This is done so that the aircraft is as close as possible to its normal weight when landing.

5. Lower your landing gear. Looks like Dad was wrong when he said you were wasting all that time playing *Microsoft Flight Simulator 98*, huh?

6. Carefully lower the aircraft to the ground. Lift up the nose so that the back wheels touch first, and then slam on the brakes once all the wheels have landed. If you managed to get this far without peeing your pants, quit your office job for something more exciting.

7. Since you're the unofficial captain, make sure all passengers and crew members are safe before you leave the aircraft.

8. Enjoy your newfound celebrity! Practice throwing a baseball because you will definitely be throwing out the first pitch at the All-Star Game.

ON WATER

1. Radio in to Ground Control to let them know you won't be landing at the airport. Just like with a dinner party, it's really rude not to let

your hosts know ahead of time. They'll send Coast Guard rescue helicopters to where you'll be crashing into the water. (This is also called "ditching.")

2. Close all air vents, valves, and any other openings that the plane may have. Planes can float on water, just not planes with water leaking into their compartments. The last thing you need when evacuating passengers from your crash-damaged plane is more holes in the plane.

3. Tell all your passengers to put on their life vests and locate the floatable life rafts before hitting the water. Otherwise it's like not using the restroom before an 800-mile road trip, but with way more hungry sharks.

4. Reduce engine power and slowly make your descent. Make sure your wings are level; if a rogue wave clips a wing, it can send the plane into a spin.

5. Get your passengers and crew off the plane as fast as possible. Even if the plane miraculously suffered no damage from the landing, water will still leak in through the doors and eventually cause it to sink.

6. Enjoy your newfound celebrity! Practice throwing a baseball because you will definitely be throwing out the first pitch at the All-Star Game.

If you crash-land on a mountain range and run out of little bags of peanuts, turn to page 148 to find out how to survive.

* * *

IF YOU CHOKE WHILE YOU'RE ALONE

Food lodged in your throat, but no one's around to administer the Heimlich maneuver? Do it yourself. Find a stationary object (like the back of a chair), and push against it with the area right above your navel. This puts pressure on the diaphragm to expel air out of the lungs and force the object out.

HOW TO STOP A RUNAWAY TRAIN

Almost all modern trains have air brakes to prevent loss of control, and all cars are connected via a brake line. In an emergency, the operator can hit a trigger that activates those brakes, stopping the train. But what if the operator passes out?

HOW TO DO IT

1. Most trains have an emergency brake in each car. It's often a cord with a handle located in a clearly labeled red box. Brace yourself for a sudden stop, and give it a good tug. If the train isn't screeching to a halt, try the one in the next car, and the one after that, and so on, as you make your way toward the engine room, a.k.a. the cab car.

2. Ask another passenger to call 911 to inform the authorities that there's an emergency. They'll contact local police and emergency

personnel, which will trigger the gates at rail crossings down the line to limit the possibility of a vehicle (or a stubborn cow) getting stuck out on the tracks.

3. If you've yanked on every emergency brake on the train and you're still moving, enter the engine room. There should be a clearly labeled "kill switch" or an "e brake" that will trigger the air brakes. If not, look for a red-colored knob or button that resembles a plunger. If you hit it repeatedly and nothing happens, try the next step.

4. It's possible that you've hit the wrong button. Look for another that might activate the brakes. Is the train still moving? Then it's safe to assume that the brakes are malfunctioning. Look for the throttle controls, typically marked by eight notches. Notch eight is the fastest speed, and notch one is the slowest. Ease the controls down, notch by notch, to notch one, and that should hopefully buy you some time and prevent the train from jumping the tracks if you go into a tight curve.

5. Find another passenger and plop him in the engine room. Have him sound the horn if a car, animal, or hobo finds his way onto the tracks up ahead.

6. With someone else at the controls, you're free to go activate the hand brakes in every car. These are typically red levers or wheels. Quickly make your way to the farthest car from the engine, and work your way back, triggering each one until the train finally, completely stops.

7. If, in the one-in-a-million chance that none of these emergency devices is working properly, move everyone to the back of the train. If it's moving slowly enough, having everyone jump off at the safest possible point might be advisable. Derailment or a crash may be inevitable at this point.

8. Now that you're officially stuck on a runaway train, get everyone back to the middle and choose a car one or two back from the center. Hopefully, there will be enough seats for everyone, because experts say that it's the

safest location during a train accident. (The worst place? The café car. Now is not the time to grab a cup of coffee and a Snickers anyway, so keep moving.)

9. Grab an aisle seat, facing the rear if possible. The authorities may use a variety of other methods not mentioned here to stop your train before it derails or crashes. If not, you should prepare for impact at any moment. Lean forward, place your hands over your head, and start praying to the deity of your choice.

TRUE TALES OF WEIRD SURVIVAL: JULIANE KOEPCKE

A HARROWING JOURNEY

In December 1971, 17-year-old Juliane Koepcke and her mother boarded LANSA flight 508 out of Lima, Peru, bound for Pucallpa, Peru. They were flying to meet Koepcke's father, a zoologist, for Christmas. The flight had been delayed for more than seven hours because of inclement weather... and it probably never should have left the airport.

Ten minutes after takeoff, the plane encountered heavy turbulence. Not much later, it was struck by lightning and from an altitude of 10,000 feet began plummeting toward the ground. The plane broke into several pieces as it fell.

Koepcke, still strapped into her seat, was sent tumbling toward the rainforest below. Amazingly, she survived the crash, with only a broken collarbone, swollen left eye, and some gashes on her arms and legs. Everyone else on board, including her mother, died on impact, or immediately after.

FINDING A WAY HOME

Now trapped in a rainforest many miles from civilization, Koepcke also realized that she had lost her glasses. Worse yet, she only had one shoe and was wearing a sleeveless minidress. Undaunted by her injuries, blurry vision, and unsuitable attire, she began using survival tactics taught to her by her father and searched for food and supplies. She found only a few pieces of candy from the plane and began a nine-day journey following a small river downstream.

At night, she couldn't sleep because of the frigid temperatures. The growing number of insect bites on her body didn't help either, nor did the maggots that began infesting her wounds from the crash. On day 10, Koepcke found an old, abandoned boat, outfitted with an engine and a can of gas. Remembering an old trick that her father had taught her, she poured gasoline on her open cuts to get rid of the maggots. She kept track of the bugs as they slipped out one by one. Her final tally: a downright horrifying 35.

Unwilling to steal the boat or risk navigating unknown waters, she waited in a nearby hut for the owners to show up. A few hours later, several Peruvian lumbermen arrived. Shocked to discover a German teenager in their hut, they first assumed that she was a half-human, half-dolphin river goddess from a local legend. (Really.) When she explained to them what had happened—in Spanish—they tended to Koepcke's wounds, got her in the boat, and drove her six miles downriver to a mill. She was quickly flown to a hospital in Pucallpa by a local pilot.

HOW TO CALM A WILD MOOSE

They may look laid-back, but these giants can be anything but gentle. Here's what to do if you ever encounter one when it's having a bad day.

• A full-grown "bull male" moose weighs in at around 1,000 pounds and stands seven feet tall. Toss in a pair of heavy antlers and you're looking at a creature that can, and will, cause a goodly amount of destruction if it's feeling cranky. Your first step to avoid a nasty run-in with a moose? Avoid them entirely. If you see a moose in the wild, walk in the other direction and keep a safe distance away.

• In North America, moose attack more humans annually than any other creature. Worldwide, only wild hippopotamuses cause more injuries. Nevertheless, moose are rarely aggressive toward people. However, if a moose feels threatened, becomes frightened, or thinks you're getting too close to its young, it will break you.

• You'll want to be especially careful while spending time in moose territory during the late spring. This is when mother moose are typically out and about with their calves and should be avoided at all costs. Males tend to be most aggressive during the fall mating season. Their bodies are raging with hormones, and many are so preoccupied with *rutting* that they stop eating for as long as a month.

• Most moose will definitely let you know if they're in a bad mood and/or ready to attack. Their ears will go back, they'll make eye contact, and they'll lower their heads in order to ram you with their antlers. They'll also likely make grunting noises, stomp their feet, claw the ground, or begin swinging their head back and forth. Should any of this unfold, turn and run away. They've made their point—most moose won't bother to chase you.

• If you encounter a male moose during mating season, however, the chances that it will give chase are far higher. Given the speediness of these creatures, running may not be practical. If you've found yourself in this scenario, put as many things between you and the moose as possible. Dart behind a tree or large rock. Climb a tree if that's an option. Wait until the moose leaves the area before heading in the opposite direction.

• If the moose manages to knock you down, protect your head with your hands and arms. *Don't* fight back. This will only encourage the moose to continue its assault. Curl up into a ball instead. Once the moose stops, wait until it moves a safe distance away before you flee. Moving too quickly could encourage it to attack again.

HOW TO MAKE UNCONVENTIONAL WEAPONS

When you've mastered the bow and arrow to the point where you could survive a Hunger Games, give one of these less conventional wilderness weapons a try.

SHEPHERD'S SLING

This is one of the oldest weapons in human history. Anthropologists think that it was first created sometime in the Upper Paleolithic era, between 12,000 and 50,000 B. C.

1. To create one of your own, you'll need a long cord made out plant fiber, roughly the length of your arm.

2. Once you've got your cord, tie a loop on one end of it (the opposite end is called the tab).

3. Next, you'll need to attach a pouch large enough to hold a rock. This can be made out

of any leftover fiber, but dried animal skin is the most suitable and durable.

4. Attach the pouch to the center of the cord.

5. Stick a rock in the pouch, and grip the loop with your thumb or forefinger, and the tab with your other fingers.

6. Raise the sling over your head and swing it rapidly. When the time is right, let go of the tab and send the rock flying in a direction that is, with any luck, nowhere near your skull.

(You're probably going to need lots of practice before you'll be able to use one effectively while defending yourself or hunting game.)

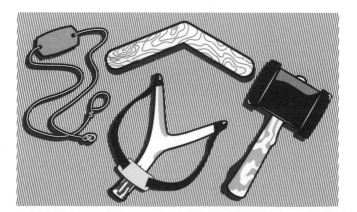

ANTLER SLINGSHOT

Why settle for a traditional slingshot when you can have one with a handle made out of an antler? However, making one of these cool "wrist rockets" will depend on whether or not you have rubber or latex tubing on hand. (An old bike tube will work, and we'll use that here as an example.)

1. You'll also need to find the right rack. Keep your eyes peeled for antlers that have been cast off as you make your way through the wilderness and/or while you're hunting big game. You'll need an antler with edges that are shaped like, well, a slingshot.

2. Break off this section, leaving enough of the antler for a handle.

3. Carve notches toward the top of each tip.

4. Slice a thin strip off the bike tube and tie one end to a notch.

5. Stretch it over to the other notch, allowing for a C-shaped strip about a foot in depth.

6. Attach a patch made out of animal skin to the center of the C, and tie the opposite end of the rubber strip to the other notch.

7. Grab a small rock, hold it against the patch, and take aim. With any luck, it won't hit you in the skull.

WAR HAMMER

This one will require basic metalsmithing skills and supplies, but you should be able to make one of these pretty wicked medieval weapons if you put your mind to it.

1. First, carve the handle out of a strong piece of wood (oak is the mightiest option) with a bracket at the top for the head. Depending on your personal preference, you can make a hammer the size of Thor's in the Marvel movies or a larger one worthy of a character from *Game of Thrones*.

2. Getting your hands on some iron in the wilderness won't be an easy task, but once you do, melt it in a sturdy pot.

3. Forge eight pins from the iron with a blunt object against a makeshift anvil (a tree trunk should work).

4. Dump them in a container of water to cool.

5. Prepare two flat iron fasteners with space in each for two pins. Toss those in the water, too.

6. Attach the fasteners to the handle by pounding four of the pins into the slots you've created.

7. Finally, forge the head with the remaining metal. Allow it to cool a bit before placing the head in the bracket of the handle.

8. Pound in the remaining pins. Allow the head to cool.

9. Carve a few totally awesome designs into the handle to strike fear into your enemies (those bears won't know what hit 'em).

10. Should your new war hammer fall apart, you can always use the handle as a club. Just don't hit yourself in the skull.

HOW TO SET A BONE ON YOUR OWN

A broken bone is no barrel of laughs under any circumstances, but in the wilderness—away from proper medical attention—the repercussions can be devastating. Even if you believe rescue is imminent, you should take immediate steps to treat a break.

BEFORE YOU BEGIN

• The jagged ends of bone can permanently damage nerves and muscle as they move around, and they can also sever blood vessels. Left unattended, even a minor break can lead to shock and sepsis.

• Fractures come in two flavors: open and closed. In an open fracture (also known as a compound fracture), broken bones protrude through the skin. This is by far the more serious of the two. But open or closed, the treatment is the same. You'll need to set the bone—that is, put it back in approximately its proper place—and then immobilize it, so it doesn't wander out of position again.

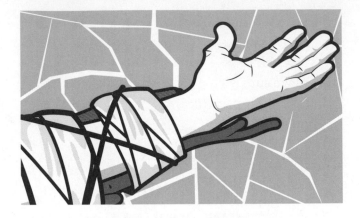

HOW TO DO IT

1. Setting a broken bone is a matter of brute force. Typically, the limb is grasped at the end above the break—that is, closer to the torso— to hold it steady, while gentle downward pressure is applied to move the limb back to its anatomically correct position. This is fine if you're treating someone else; but if you're alone, you will have neither sufficient leverage nor the free hand to do the job. You need to reverse the usual process here, holding the limb stable below the break and aligning the upper portion.

2. Look for someplace stable where you can wedge the limb to hold it steady; a forking tree trunk, perhaps, or a crevice in a rock face. Make sure it's not so narrow that you'll get stuck. Wrap the limb in a shirt or jacket to protect it.

3. Once the limb is secure, lean back carefully, using your body weight, and twist to line up the broken portions of the limb. There shouldn't be much resistance while you're doing this. In an open fracture, the bones will generally slide back under the skin as you reposition.

4. If you encounter undue resistance, stop what you're doing and splint the limb as it lies; never try to force the bone to go somewhere it doesn't want to go. Now, this is going to hurt while you're doing it—a lot. But once the bone's back in place, it will actually relieve your discomfort.

5. Immobilize the limb with a splint. Any rigid material will do—tent poles, canoe paddles, scrap wood, even cardboard. Splint the limb

on two sides to keep it motionless. Secure with bootlaces, belts, duct tape—whatever's at hand—fastening snugly but not tightly. Check for circulation, sensation, and movement in the limb; if you lose feeling or color, loosen the splint binding. After the break is secure, you can treat an open fracture as you would any open wound.

* * *

SPIN CYCLE

In May 2011, a tornado was roaring through Lenox, Iowa, when 11-year-old Austin Miller got a call from his mother, Jessica, who was at work: "Get in the laundry room NOW!" Jessica tried to drive home, but her way was blocked by a wall of debris, so she took shelter in her mother-in-law's cellar. After the tornado passed, she ran to her own house. The roof had collapsed, and there was no sign of Austin. Just then, the clothes-dryer door popped open and out he came. He had squeezed in just in time to ride out the storm.

HOW TO DEAL WITH A RABID DOG

Rabies is infectious, excruciating, and lethal. It's caused by a virus and transmitted by biting. It attacks the brain, and an affected dog will be hyperreactive and snap at anything nearby. Here's how to make sure it doesn't snap at you.

HOW TO DO IT

1. There's no way to sweeten this: Your best chance at survival is to straight-up kill this dog. Take a moment to deal with the emotional ramifications of that.

2. If you are unarmed, you'll have to neutralize the dog. Grab an umbrella or a stick, the longer the better. In a pinch, you can use a sweatshirt or jacket.

3. Wave your stick at the dog to draw its jaws away from you and your fleshier parts.

4. Once the dog bites down on the stick, move quickly. Step in beside the dog, placing your free hand or knee on the back of its neck.

5. Drop down with all your weight while simultaneously jerking the stick upward, breaking the dog's neck.

6. Take a moment to grieve, both for the dog and for the loss of your innocence. Console yourself with the knowledge that a quick, relatively painless death is a mercy to the dog, in the long run.

7. Even if you are not bitten, seek medical attention immediately. The dog's saliva is loaded with the rabies virus, so you'll want to rule out any chance of infection.

* * *

THE BEST SURVIVAL TIP

Rule #1 for any catastrophe: *Stay calm.* Easier said than done? Not really. If your car careens off a cliff, you may think that you'll scream all the way down. But many people who have survived disasters report that time slows down and the mind clicks into a serene clarity of purpose. So, follow your surprising instincts...and don't freak out.

HOW TO PERFORM A TRACHEOTOMY

Here's what to do if you're with someone who can't breathe—at all—and nothing else works. The good news is that it's probably not going to be as bloody as you think it will be.

WHAT YOU'LL NEED

- A razor blade, or a very sharp knife
- A straw, or a ballpoint pen with the ink tube removed
- Disinfectant for those tools (but time is of the essence, so make it snappy)

HOW TO DO IT

1. Undertake this procedure only if a few conditions are met. Is there in an object stuck in your friend's throat that is preventing airflow of any kind? If he can't even gasp or cough, he might need a tracheotomy.

2. Nevertheless, since this is minor, albeit

on-the-fly, surgery, you don't want to do it if you don't have to. Perform the Heimlich maneuver three times. If you can't dislodge the object at fault, proceed with the tracheotomy.

3. Have the patient lie down on his back…if he hasn't already passed out.

4. Locate the small indentation that sits between two lumps on the throat: the cricoid cartilage and the Adam's apple. (If your patient is female, she won't have an Adam's apple. Simply locate the other bulge, and then the indentation will be right there.)

5. On the depression, use the razor blade or sharp knife to make a horizontal cut. It should be as wide as it is deep: about a half an inch both ways.

6. Carefully pinch the incision, or stick your finger into the hole to widen it and open it up, ever so slightly.

7. Insert the straw or ballpoint pen tube into the incision. Don't push too far—it only needs to go in about as far as you made the initial cut.

8. Breathe into the tube with two quick breaths. Wait five seconds, and then breathe into it every five seconds until breathing resumes.

9. The person will begin to breathe on his or her own again and, if applicable, regain consciousness.

10. Call the paramedics.

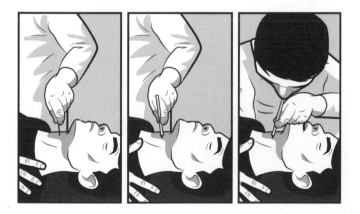

HOW TO MAKE (AND USE) PRISON WEAPONRY

So you messed up and landed yourself in the Big House. Nah, don't bother telling us you're innocent. The thing is, kid, good or bad, you're going to need some protection.

WHAT YOU'LL NEED

- Toothbrush
- Cigarettes
- Lighter
- Magazines
- Dental floss
- Bar soap
- Socks
- Canned food

HOW TO DO IT

1. **Know the lingo.** A *shiv* is a sharp blade for slicing—e.g., a razor. A *shank* is for stabbing; it has a point, but no edge as such. Decide which jailhouse weapon is right for you.

2. **Know when and why to use a weapon.** Jailhouse violence is rarely spontaneous.

Forget about carrying a blade everywhere for "self-defense." You'll go armed only when the situation requires: when your prison gang declares war on another prison gang, when you're tapped to deliver a message, or when you've got a score to settle.

3. **Keep it disposable.** Being caught with a weapon could earn you up to a year in solitary confinement, so you'll want a weapon that's made for the job at hand and easily discarded afterward. You can fashion a shank from a toothbrush in a matter of minutes simply by scraping the handle against a rough surface to give it a point. If your unit allows inmates access to canned food, the jagged edge of a can top makes for an excellent shiv.

4. **Think nonlethal.** If your intention is simple assault, a blackjack is the weapon of choice. Stuff a bar of soap into a sock for a beatdown that gets your message across...without drawing blood.

5. **Get creative.** Everything's a potential weapon in prison. Light a cigarette filter on

fire, and the cellulose acetate fibers melt into a small plastic shard that will hold an edge. Tightly rolled magazines are just as rigid as a broom handle, and can be attached to a shank to create a crude spear—giving you the reach to attack a guard through the bars.

6. **Time is your greatest resource.** Guys have been known to cut jagged shards of sheet steel out of their bunks using nothing but dental floss! Sure, it took months, even years. But time is all you have in prison.

* * *

HOW TO ENDURE AN EARTHQUAKE

Do not stand in a doorway. The best place to be is far from windows, glass, and precarious, heavy objects. That might mean standing against an interior wall. Go to your closest safe spot, drop to the ground (preferably under a large desk), and protect your head. If you're in bed, stay there and hold a pillow over your head. If an earthquake hits while you're driving, stop the car away from power lines, trees, and overpasses, and stay there.

HOW NOT TO GET EATEN

*Fantastic beasts, and where to avoid them,
so as not to get eaten by them.*

CROCODILES

Crocodiles are some of nature's most ruthless (and quiet) killers. While hunting, they can stealthily move through water with only their eyes and nostrils visible. Gustave, a 2,000-pound crocodile that roams the northern banks of Lake Tanganyika in eastern Africa, is believed to have killed as many as 300 people.

If you don't want to wind up in a croc's jaws, the most obvious thing to do is avoid riverbanks and other waterways where crocodiles are native. *Don't go in the water unless you absolutely must.* Set up your camp well away from lakes and rivers, and don't leave any food out. If you spot a croc, make a break for it—the world's fastest crocodiles can only run about 10 mph, and they tire quickly while on land. If it attacks, fight back by clawing at its eyes or nostrils.

COUGARS

These large cats, also known as mountain lions or catamounts, prefer to dine on wild deer and moose. In most cases, they'll only attack a human if they feel threatened. If you get on a cougar's bad side, *don't run or attempt to play dead*. This could kickstart their natural instinct to chase their prey and/or mark you as an easy target. Instead, make yourself seem as threatening as possible. Stick out your chest, wave your arms around, and start screaming. (What you say doesn't matter, but you could say that dogs are better than cats, or that its mother was less than purr-fect, for example.) Throw sticks or rocks at the cougar if you can.

If it attacks, protect your neck, literally—it'll instinctively go for your jugular. Again, don't play dead. Fight back with everything you've got. If you manage to scare the cougar away, you're not out of the woods yet—literally and figuratively. The cougar may track you for miles hoping that you'll succumb to your injuries. Get to safety as quickly as possible. One more tip: Cougars are most active at dawn and dusk, so you might want to lie low during these hours.

POLAR BEARS

Global climate change is gravely impacting these beasts, and their habitat is disappearing. This means they'll happily make a meal out of you, especially if they can't find a delicious seal or a blubbery walrus carcass. Polar bears are the world's largest and most powerful land carnivores, so you're unlikely to survive a close encounter with one if its stomach is grumbling or if it has hungry cubs to feed. Desperate polar bears have been known to track humans long distances and attack Arctic research camps and rural outposts in the dead of night. If you're stuck way, way up north with limited resources, setting up a rudimentary trip warning system for your camp would be advisable, but you're unlikely to find the necessary components in the frozen wastes. If you're with companions, organize a night watch and make weapons out of whatever is available (see page 210).

Go for the bear's eyes or throat if it attacks. However, if one of them gets close enough to sink its teeth into your flesh, you can probably kiss your butt good-bye. Running probably won't do you any good, either: the average full-grown polar bear can gallop as fast as a horse.

CHIPMUNKS

There's about a one-in-a-million chance you'll ever have your life threatened by a chipmunk, but, hey, better safe than sorry. Many people assume that these adorable rodents eat only nuts and berries. Wrong. They're omnivorous and have been known to consume insects, worms, small species of frogs, and even the occasional bird egg. If, in the highly unlikely event that you encounter a rabid chipmunk or one that has developed a taste for human flesh, you probably won't be able to outrun it. Chipmunks are notoriously speedy and can dash up to 21 mph. On the other hand, if one dive-bombs you from a tree or starts gnawing on your leg, you could simply pry it off and fling it into the woods.

Fending off one or two vicious chipmunks should be a simple task for the average healthy adult, but what if you're attacked by a dozen or more? (Hey, it could happen.) Use the tactics that have been outlined elsewhere in this article. Try to scare them away by screaming and looking as dangerous as possible. If they swarm, protect your neck and eyes at all costs. Stop, drop, and roll to crush or injure your attackers, especially if they run up your pant legs or manage to infiltrate the clothing covering your upper torso. Make removing the chipmunks from your face and neck a priority. Their teeth aren't terribly sharp, so it will take them a good deal of time to inflict damage on the rest of your body.

TRUE TALES OF WEIRD SURVIVAL: WILLIAM RANKIN

OH, CHUTE

Of all the harsh environments you might find yourself trying to survive in, it's hard to imagine anywhere you are more helpless than in a free fall... during a thunderstorm...for 40 minutes.

Lt. Col. William Rankin and another pilot were each flying an F-8 Crusader fighter jet over North Carolina in July 1959. They climbed to 47,000 feet to get above a cumulonimbus thunderstorm cloud, and the gathering storm below. As they prepared to begin their descent, Rankin heard a rumble in his engines. The power went out, and a warning light signaled fire. He tried to restart the engines, to no avail, and the plane plunged into the cloud at nearly supersonic speed. This made "ejecting into a thunderstorm" his best option.

KEEPIN' COOL

The air outside the plane was –50°F, causing instant frostbite. The rapid decompression at that altitude caused Rankin's abdomen to swell, and he immediately began bleeding from anywhere exposed that he could bleed from: his eyes, ears, nose, and mouth. Only the oxygen canister attached to his helmet allowed him to keep breathing and remain alert.

From an altitude of nine miles above the earth, Rankin knew it would take a little more than three minutes of free fall before he reached an altitude that would trigger the automatic release on his parachute. He checked his watch. After four minutes, his chute still hadn't deployed, and Rankin worried it had malfunctioned, so he pulled the chute manually.

LIFE IN HAIL

What Rankin didn't realize was that the massive updraft within the thundercloud was slowing his descent, which was why his chute hadn't deployed on its own. As soon as he released it, the updraft on the parachute pulled him back up higher into the cloud at nearly 100 miles per hour.

He was pelted with hail, and the air was so thick with water that he had to hold his breath for fear he would drown. The only break in the darkness came from frequent bursts of lightning, which Rankin said looked like blue blades several feet thick.

When the updraft ran out of steam, Rankin began falling again, tangled in his parachute. Miraculously, he was able to untangle himself from the chute, only to be pulled up by another updraft. And so the cycle continued, with Rankin being pulled up into the cloud and then falling with his chute tangled around him. It was like a Wile E. Coyote cartoon, although Rankin probably didn't see the humor at the time.

Finally, the storm weakened, and on one of his downward trajectories, Rankin descended all the way to the ground in a North Carolina forest. He looked at his watch. It was nearly 40 minutes after he had ejected from the plane. Covered in blood and vomit, and suffering from decompression shock, he wandered to a nearby road. Someone stopped and picked him up. After three weeks in the hospital, Rankin was released and resumed his military career as a pilot.

HOW TO MAKE TOOLS FROM ANIMAL BONES

This pretty gross activity went out of style in the Bronze Age, but if you're in a desperate situation, there's nothing wrong with reaching for the nearest femur to turn it into a makeshift hammer.

WHAT YOU'LL NEED

- One deer or elk, preferably dead
- A strong rock to serve as your hammer stone
- A smaller but equally strong rock that can be used as a wedge
- A third rock that you'll use as a chisel
- A few horsetail plants

HOW TO DO IT

1. First, you'll need to hunt down an animal, the larger the better. While a battle axe made out of a bear humerus might look totally wicked (and strike fear into the hearts of

your enemies), you may want to aim for a deer or an elk instead. Native American tribes from all across North America once swore by them and considered these large mammals a living hardware store of tools just waiting to be freed.

2. Once you've bagged your furry tool kit, bring it back to your camp and clean the carcass using the methods outlined on page 160. If you're using a deer or elk to make your new awl, grab a cannon bone—it's the one beneath the knee.

3. Don't dillydally. The fresher the bone, the easier it will be to turn into a tool. Older bones tend to be tougher and require a lot more elbow grease.

4. Find your hammer stone and start pounding away on each end of the bone, not unlike those apes from the beginning of *2001: A Space Odyssey*. But don't get too carried away—you don't want to pound your bone into dust. Once the ends are gone and you can see down into the hollow interior, move on to the next step.

5. Grab your chisel and create a groove down both sides of the bone. Find a comfy spot to sit before you begin. This step will probably require an hour or more of steady scrapping.

6. Position the wedge so that its edges match up with the grooves.

7. Now start tapping on it as if you were chopping a piece of wood...but don't hit it too hard. A gentle but firm stroke should do the trick. Those grooves should gradually turn

into cracks and snap. Keep going until the bone has been split into two equal pieces.

8. Use your hammer stone to break off a section of bone that is sized to your preference. Then scrape one edge along an abrasive surface until it's whittled down into a sharp point. Note: this could take a good chunk of time.

9. Grab one of those horsetails and use it to further hone the point (it'll also give your new tool a nice polish). Ta-da! You've just made an awl that you can use to make a cool belt or a very stylish vest out of a dried animal skin. You should have plenty of deer hide left over for both garments, right?

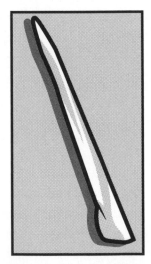

10. Now that you've got yourself a brand-new awl, you shouldn't stop there. You can make all sorts of awesome tools out of the rest of those deer bones.

HOW TO PERFORM AN EXORCISM

Actual statistics are hard to come by, but we can all agree that a certain number of people each year are possessed by demonic spirits. If it happens to someone you love, you may have no choice but to perform a Catholic-style exorcism.

• **Ideally, an exorcism should be performed by a priest or some other ordained member of the clergy.** However, if this isn't possible, you can do it yourself. You'll need to start by purifying yourself, and your soul, as much as possible. A good way to start is to go to confession. Be sure to fess up to the *really* dark stuff, and be genuinely sorry for it.

• **Before you begin your exorcism, make sure the afflicted person is actually possessed and not dealing with some other (and eminently more treatable) psychological condition.** Now, *some* people will tell you that people who believe in exorcism are themselves suffering from delusions, but don't let them dissuade you. They are probably under the influence of a demon themselves.

• **The traditional attire for an exorcism is a white surplice with a purple stole**...in other words, a white tunic and a purple scarf. But do the best you can with whatever you have on hand. Will the clothes you wear really make an impact on the demon? It's hard to say.

• **If the possessed person is thrashing about or refuses to remain still,** you may have to tie him or her down or otherwise restrain the poor soul. Take care not to injure the possessed person.

• **The actual ritual of exorcism is essentially a prayer** to God, Jesus, and the Holy Spirit, asking all of them to come together to expel the demon from the possessed person. You've got some creative license in how exactly you express your prayer. Don't be afraid to just ask directly in plain speech, "Please get this demon out of my friend Barry!" It's also common to recite the Litany of the Saints, a lengthy prayer that invokes the name of all of the ordained saints, often asking them to "have mercy on us" and "hear us."

• **Holy objects can also be used to help expel the demon.** The two most common tools are a cross and holy water. Simply show the possessed person the cross and occasionally sprinkle the afflicted with holy water as you recite your prayers. If you don't have these objects on hand, just make the sign of the cross to yourself and over the possessed person.

• **Don't be discouraged if the exorcism doesn't work right away.** Sometimes it will take a course of exorcisms over a period of weeks or months, sort of like physical therapy.

* * *

TOO COLD/TOO HOT

Normal internal body temperature is 98.6°F (37°C). If a person's body temperature falls below 85°F (29°C), the chances of survival are doubtful; at 80°F (26°C), coma sets in, and death is pretty much assured once body temp dips to 70°F (21°C). On the high end, only a few people have survived a body temperature above 112°F (44°C).

HOW TO NEGOTIATE A HOSTAGE SITUATION

Some individual or group is holding people against their will and threatening to kill them if their demands aren't met. But if you believe in yourself, you too can negotiate a hostage situation. (Note: Not really. Don't be an idiot. Leave this to the FBI.)

HOW TO DO IT

1. **Make contact with the hostage taker(s) and establish yourself as the contact for negotiations.** Often, this is done over the phone. While you will be their contact person, it's important that you are just an intermediary, not also the person with the authority to grant their demands. This allows you to at least appear impartial, and it gives you a useful stalling technique while you purport to consult with officials on the outside.

2. **Find out everything you can about who is inside.** How many captors and hostages are there? Where are they? Are any of them injured? This information will be crucial as you plan your strategy.

3. **Determine what happened that led to the hostages being taken and what the captors want to release them.** Some hostage situations are unplanned, the result of a spur-of-the-moment decision in something like a domestic altercation, or an attempt to avoid capture after something like a botched robbery. These people are

often flustered and unsure of what they want. Other times, particularly if the motives are political, the assailants have planned to create a hostage situation and will have very specific demands already in mind.

4. **Develop a rough psychological profile of the hostage taker.** Is he or she a mentally ill person behaving irrationally? A cool political operative with a firm agenda? The better you understand who the hostage taker is and what their motivations are, the better you will be able to make progress in the negotiations and avoid triggers that could lead the captor to harm hostages.

5. **Prolong the situation and keep things calm.** The longer a hostage situation lasts, the better the odds that it will end peacefully. Pretend to be interested in whatever the hostage takers want to discuss, and ask lots of open-ended questions to keep them talking. Once the hostage takers have made demands, stall by telling them you're waiting for an answer yourself from the folks in charge.

6. **Build empathy between yourself and the hostage takers, and between the hostage takers and the hostages.** At the beginning of a hostage situation, the hostages are merely bargaining chips. The more you can make the hostage takers see them as human beings, the less likely the captors will be to kill them. If you can get the hostage takers to accept things like food or medicine for the hostages, distributing them will force the captors to engage in a caring, communal act with the hostages.

7. **Make small concessions to chip away at their demands.** In some cases, it may be possible to meet the hostage takers' demands, particularly if they are demanding ransom and there is a party willing to pay it. Often, however, it will not be advisable or even possible to meet their demands. Try to offer small things, particularly amenities like food and water. If they are politically motivated, you may be able to offer them something like media attention. You may be able to broker the release of a prisoner or two for each concession—and even if you can't do that, you

will be prolonging the situation and building empathy.

8. **The final result is out of your hands.** As a hostage negotiator, you can build empathy, try to broker prisoner releases in exchange for concessions, and prolong the situation to try to foster a positive outcome. But the final resolution will be determined either by the hostage takers, who decide to give up or kill the hostages, or by the authorities, who may decide to go in and try to capture the criminals. So don't sweat it! You did the best you could.

* * *

NUMBER TWO DISASTER

In 2015, 73 acres of forest outside Boise, Idaho, were destroyed by wildfire. An investigation revealed the cause: A cyclist traveling in the area didn't want to leave behind his used toilet paper, so he burned it. But an ember escaped, caught some dry grass, and spread.

DANGEROUS ADVICE!

Outdated survival guides and old movies spread a lot of misinformation that might just get you killed. Here are some of the craziest bits of advice we found that you simply shouldn't heed.

MOST WILD MUSHROOMS ARE TOTALLY FINE

Plenty of books out there will teach you what fungus among us is safe to eat. And there are quite a few tasty varieties to be found in the woods, far more than will poison or kill you if you eat them.

However, the photos and pictures in these books don't always match up with what you'll find in the wild. It's incredibly easy to mistake, say, a couple of dangerous orange-colored *Omphalotus olearius* (a.k.a. "Jack o' Lantern mushrooms) for some incredibly tasty orange-colored chanterelles. Unless you're an expert when it comes to this sort of thing, or very desperate, you're better off searching for other sources of food in the wild.

A ROOF OVER YOUR HEAD IS ALL THAT MATTERS

Tons of survival guides will tell you how to build a shelter out of everything from rocks to snow. (Including this one! Please turn to page 134.) Unfortunately, few of them also note that having a roof over your head is only half the battle when it comes to braving the elements. (But this one does. Please keep reading this page.) While shelter will help keep rain and hail directly off you, it won't prevent you from freezing to death on a frigid night. Sleeping on cold ground can and will suck the life-giving body heat right out of you. A bed, a makeshift mattress, or any soft surface that will help keep you warm is equally important.

AVOID A RIP CURRENT BY SWIMMING PARALLEL TO THE SHORE

If you did this, in all likelihood, you'd just tucker yourself out and then drown. It's better to swim perpendicular to the direction of the prevailing tide or wind. Once you escape the riptide, swim at an angle away from it toward dry land.

YOU CAN COOK BREAKFAST IN A BAG

At least one old outdoor guide claims that you can cook bacon and eggs in a paper bag. Supposedly, the grease from the food will gradually coat the inside of the bag and prevent it from bursting into flames. According to the guide, all you need to do is stick everything in the bag, place it on some hot coals, and wait a while before digging in. Uh... no. Unless your coals are the absolute perfect temperature (good luck with that), the paper will almost certainly ignite—grease isn't a fire retardant as much as it is a fire igniter.

HOW TO ESCAPE FROM QUICKSAND

Whatever you think you know about quicksand you probably learned from the movies, but the real physics of quicksand are a lot weirder.

BREAKING THE SURFACE

Quicksand isn't sand—it's a gel that forms when sand becomes saturated with water and creates a colloidal suspension. It's not dissolved, but the particles are dispersed through the water such that they don't settle, making a spongy, semisolid surface. When surface tension is disrupted, as by a person attempting to walk on it, the suspension breaks, and the gel separates into liquid water and pockets of dense, compacted sediment.

DON'T STRUGGLE

Quicksand pits simply aren't deep enough to pull you under, but those sediment pockets act like thick mud puddles, the kind that can suck your boot right off. If your foot gets stuck, you'll have to expend a thousand pounds of force to pull it free. The real danger is that you'll exhaust yourself in the effort and then drown in three feet of water.

STAY BUOYANT

Lie slowly backward, taking care not to splash around. Gradually spread your arms wide. Don't try to lift your feet, but slowly spread them. Allow yourself to float: The water/sand suspension is denser than ordinary water, and will bear you up. Gently backstroke your way toward solid ground. When you reach the edge, pull yourself out of the quicksand using only your arms, letting your legs float behind you.

HOW TO FAKE YOUR OWN DEATH

Whether you've got a bunch of debt you don't want to pay or you're on the run from the Yakuza, you gotta do what you gotta do.

HOW TO DO IT

1. Leave trace remains of your "dead" body: hair, teeth, maybe even a bloody pinky if you're really taking this seriously. (Faking your own death is not the time to do something halfway.)

2. Don't tell your family. If you're really serious about starting a new life, your immediate family members will only be a liability. So make the most of your precious time left with your mother-in-law and weird cousin Al from Spokane.

3. Go entirely off the grid. In the old days, that meant not paying rent with your old checkbook, but today it's much harder. That

means no smartphones with built-in GPS, no pulling cash out of ATMs, and no using the library's computer to leave mean Internet comments.

4. Don't use a huge event to fake your own death. While it seems shrewd, it's much easier to get caught when teams of federal agents are investigating the incident. For example, Steven Chin Leung's "brother" told a federal judge that Leung was consulting in Cantor Fitzgerald's WTC offices on 9/11. But after a short investigation, law enforcement discovered that Leung was alive, and was simply trying to avoid his upcoming trial for passport fraud.

5. Withdraw as much money as possible, as gradually as possible. You're going to need cash to sustain yourself until you find a new job, but withdrawing it all in one trip to the bank will raise red flags with your bank and anybody else on your account. Anyway, your ATM's daily withdrawal limit is probably under six figures.

6. Create a new identity. Your new persona should be entirely different from the life you once led. For example, if you accidentally blow up your commanding officer during the Korean War, steal his identity and become a handsome advertising creative director in 1960s Manhattan.

7. Stock up on grub. It's best to avoid human contact unless absolutely necessary, so replace your weekly trip to the market with self-replenishing food: Fruit and veggies that give off seeds and egg-producing livestock like chicken. If you want fish, you better move to a lake. Buying a gigantic aquarium isn't the best idea for staying low-key.

8. Get rid of this book! Now, we'd never recommend destroying the fine work of the Bathroom Readers' Institute, but you don't want the local authorities to come across a book with dog-eared pages and underlined tips in the section called "How to Fake Your Own Death." So before your untimely "passing," donate it your local thrift shop so another person can fake their own death.

HOW TO BUY A BATHROOM READER AND WIN!

Contact us at:
Bathroom Readers' Institute
P.O. Box 1117
Ashland, OR 97520

THE LAST PAGE

Fellow Bathroom Readers:

The fight for good bathroom reading should never be taken loosely—we must do our duty and sit firmly for what we believe in, even while the rest of the world is taking potshots at us.

We'll be brief. Now that we've proven we're not simply a flush-in-the-pan, we invite you to take the plunge:

Sit Down and Be Counted! Log on to *www.bathroomreader.com* and earn a permanent spot on the BRI honor roll!

If you like reading our books...VISIT THE BRI'S WEBSITE!
www.bathroomreader.com

- Receive our irregular newsletters via e-mail
- Order additional Bathroom Readers
- Face us on Facebook
- Tweet us on Twitter
- Blog us on our blog

Go with the Flow...

Well, we're out of space, and when you've gotta go, you've gotta go. Tanks for all your support.
Hope to hear from you soon.

Meanwhile, remember...

KEEP ON FLUSHIN'!